Library of Industrial and Commercial Edu

ADVISORY EDITORS:

B. H. Henson, B.Sc.(Econ.) and T. F. West, D.Sc.

CATERING DIVISION

General Editors: J. Murphy and J. Collar

MENU TERMINOLOGY

MENU TERMINOLOGY

BY

HAROLD C. CLARKE, M.H.C.I.

(Lecturer, Food Studies Dept., Garnett College of Education, London S.W.15.)

PERGAMON PRESS

OXFORD · NEW YORK
TORONTO · SYDNEY · BRAUNSCHWEIG

PERGAMON PRESS LIMITED
OXFORD · NEW YORK
TORONTO · SYDNEY · BRAUNSCHWEIG

First edition 1969

Reprinted 1975

Library of Congress Catalog Card No. 78-86532

Printed in Great Britain by Biddles Ltd., Guildford, Surrey.

08 006525 2 (flexicover)

Contents

Foreword

I WELCOME the idea of Harold C. Clarke of collecting together in one handy volume a glossary of culinary terms, their origins and uses. I particularly recommend it to the student of cuisine who will find it invaluable, not only during his years of apprenticeship in the art of haute cuisine, but also as a handy reference book throughout his career.

Unlike almost every other trade or profession, international cuisine is universal, and abiding by the correct terminology when making menus and producing dishes it is essential to follow the classical recipe. Modern diet is perhaps less elaborate than, say, in the days of Carême and Escoffier. Therefore if ingredients are varied the name of the dish should be altered.

EUGÈNE KAUFELER

Preface

THIS book had its origin from a special study, prepared by the writer whilst studying at Garnett College, London, for the Teacher's Certificate of the Institute of Education, London University.

Prior to this period, I had been engaged in the teaching of courses leading to the City and Guilds of London Institute's examinations for the Hotel and Catering Industry, particularly 151. The syllabus of the City and Guilds 151 and 152 courses requires students undertaking these examinations to have an adequate knowledge of culinary terms and garnishes. In addition, students should gain some understanding of the derivation of dishes. Reference books for this aspect of the syllabus, particularly historical origins, appeared to me to be rather limited, although many include some information on this subject. For this reason I chose this particular topic in the hope that such a book might help to fulfil this need.

I am indebted to Miss M. Todd, F.H.C.I., M.I.M.A., Principal Lecturer in Food Studies at Garnett College, and to Miss K. M. Griffin, F.H.C.I., Head of Department of Catering at the South East London Technical College, for their help and encouragement in the preparation of this book. I should also like to express my appreciation to those authors whose works I have consulted and to my former colleagues at the South East London Technical College and Henley College of Further Education, Coventry; in particular to Miss P. M. Dingley, for her help in the drafting of the manuscript.

I am grateful to the Dorchester Hotel, Limited, for their permission to reproduce the menus at the end of the book and to

PREFACE

Eugène Kaufeler, Maître Chef des Cuisines at the Dorchester Hotel, for his assistance.

I also appreciate the guidance and assistance I have received from Pergamon Press Ltd. (Publishers).

Publisher's Foreword

THE Industrial Training Act has resulted in an increase in the number of people now being trained or re-trained. LICET books are intended to provide suitable texts which will be easy to read and assimilate for those employed in industry and commerce who are receiving further education and training as a part of their employment. It is hoped that they will be particularly suitable for those attending courses leading to the examinations of the City and Guilds of London Institute, the Regional Examining Unions and other examining bodies.

The books are essentially straightforward, simple and practical in their approach and are designed to provide all the basic knowledge required for a particular trade or occupation. They are structured in such a way that the subject is broken down into convenient and progressive components, and are written by authors specially chosen for their expert knowledge and for their practical and teaching experience of their subjects.

Where appropriate, emphasis has been placed on safety training. In some subjects separate manuals on safety and safety training will be provided; in other texts, authors have been encouraged to emphasize safety precautions at relevant points, or to devote a separate chapter to these matters.

LICET books are published in a number of subject divisions, with each division controlled by a specialist editor responsible for selecting authors and providing guidance and advice to both authors and publisher. It is hoped that the series will make an important contribution to further education and industrial training.

ROBERT MAXWELL
Publisher

CHAPTER 1

Introduction

THE language used in the composition of hotel and restaurant menus has been influenced by many factors. A classical menu features names of dishes which can be interpreted precisely by chefs and gastronomes. An endeavour has been made by the writer to explain the meaning of some of the language used, including the history and origins of names of dishes.

Originally a menu was not a "bill of fare", as we know it today. In old French it was called an "escriteau" and was merely a card bearing the list of food to be prepared. The purpose was to give instructions to the kitchen staff and to keep a record of the food consumed.

The individual menu, in use today, was not introduced until the early nineteenth century. These menus in addition to indicating the choice of food available to the customer, also form the basic plan of the organization of the kitchen. It is often suggested that there are too many different names of dishes used in the compilation of menus. In answer to this I would say that the value of having specific names, most of which are included in Saulinier's *Le Répertoire de la Cuisine*, lies in the lack of ambiguity in the language used, which is essential to the customer and to chefs, in order that accuracy and clarity may prevail. Doubtless, a menu written in French is sometimes puzzling to customers. However, this is easily overcome by providing a clear concise explanation in English of each item on the menu as is customary in many English hotels.

Although there has been much argument within the Hotel and

Catering Industry in recent years, concerning the use of French in the composition of menus in more modest establishments, few would dispute its continued use as the international language of the "cuisine" in first-class hotels, and in tourist centres of the world.

The development of menu language was the result, many years ago, of an awareness by former dedicated craftsmen of the kitchen, of the need for some standardization in the many dishes offered on restaurant menus. It became increasingly important, especially as people travelled more widely, for informed diners throughout the world to be able to associate dishes by virtue of their principal ingredients and method of presentation, with their name on a menu, irrespective of where they were served. Menu language became naturally associated with the French language, owing to the part played by French chefs in the development of professional cookery. Although items in the culinary repertoire have derived from a number of sources, many of them have been modified or perfected by chefs, of whom many were French. It should not be forgotten, however, that the Italians were responsible for much of the early practising of the culinary arts; Catherine de Médicis, wife of Henry II of France, introduced Italian cooks into the French Court, who then instructed the French in the art of cooking.

The French used (on menus) is virtually a technical language which has become internationally adopted. Many of the terms associated with cookery processes are unable to be translated, and it is for this reason that the first section of this book has been devoted to the use of words and terms which are featured in menu language. The terms defined are generally those which actually appear on menus, rather than the many others which are used in the kitchen to describe some culinary methods and preparations, except where necessary in order to clarify other entries. A vocabulary of certain less common items of food has also been included in the first section. Terms which are defined in this study are French, unless otherwise stated.

In cases of doubt concerning the composition of garnishes I have adhered to Escoffier's *Guide to Modern Cookery* or to Saulnier's *Le Répertoire de la Cuisine*.

CHAPTER 2

Culinary Terms and Vocabulary

Agneau de lait. A baby lamb which is wholly milk fed, "agneau de Pauillac" is one of the best known varieties.

Aiguillettes. The term can refer to small strips of cooked meats and to small fillets of fish, e.g. "aiguillettes de sole". The breasts of ducks and geese are carved "en aiguillette".

Aile. The wing of a bird, for example, pheasant, "aile de faisan".

Aloyau. A sirloin of beef, which includes part of the rump, the sirloin and the fillet. The sirloin is said to owe its name to King Charles II, who after eating some of a loin of beef and being extremely satisfied with it, asked the name of the joint. When he was told, he said, "For its merit then, I will knight it and henceforth it shall be called Sir Loin."[1] In fact this colourful anecdote is inaccurate as the word sirloin is derived from the French "surlonge".

Arcanette. A small teal of real gastronomic merit, peculiar to the Lorraine marshlands.

Baba. A Polish cake brought to the French Court by the daughter of the Polish King Stanislas Leczinski; the name is said to come from the Polish word "babka". A "baba" is prepared from a rich yeast dough, usually containing currants, it is often flavoured with rum.

Ballotine. These are small balls or rolls of meat or poultry, i.e. "Ballotine de volaille". The term may also be applied to a boned, stuffed duck, "Ballotine de canard".

[1] Senn, C. Herman, *Dictionary of Foods*, Ward Lock, London.

3

Baron. A double sirloin of beef or a saddle of lamb or mutton with legs attached.

Bisque. It is the name of a cream soup which is prepared from shellfish, i.e. crayfish, "bisque d'écrevisse", or lobster, "bisque d'homard". In former times the name applied to a preparation of game or poultry, which was thickened with pulverized toast or biscuit, from which it derives its name.

Blanquette. As applied to a "blanquette de veau" takes its name from the French "blanc" meaning white. A "blanquette" is a white stew, usually of veal or lamb, in which the meat is masked with a white sauce, which is prepared from the cooking liquor and finished with a liaison of yolks of eggs and cream.

Blinis. This is a type of Russian pancake prepared from buckwheat flour; it is served with caviare.

Bombe. An iced sweet prepared in a bomb-shaped mould. The mould is usually lined with various flavoured ices, the centre is filled with a cream and fruit preparation or ice-creams.

Bonne-bouche. A name given to small savoury dishes, also to hot "hors d'œuvre".

Bouchées. These are small puff paste patties which are meant to be a mouthful only, from the French "bouche" meaning mouth. They may be filled with a preparation of chicken, ham, mushrooms or shell-fish.

Brioche. A light cake made from a yeast dough, usually in the shape of a circle surmounted by a head. The name "brioche" is said to have derived from two old French words, "bris" meaning to break and "hocher" meaning to stir, which together have resulted in the word "brioche".

Capon. A chicken which has an undrawn weight of 6–9 lb. It is a cock-bird which is specially treated with hormones and fattened for roasting.

Charlotte. A hot or cold sweet dish of which there are many varieties, e.g. Apple Charlotte. Charlotte is believed to be a corruption of the very old English word "charlyt" which meant a dish of custard.

Civet. This word applies particularly to "ragoûts" of fûrred game, especially hare, i.e. "Civet de lièvre". The term "civet" comes from the French "cive" meaning green onion, because in the past this dish was flavoured with these onions. In the preparation of jugged hare, the meat is marinaded in red wine and olive oil, flavoured with aromates, preferably for 48 hours. A brown stew is prepared, the marinade is added when moistening with the stock. This dish is usually garnished with button onions, turned mushrooms and lardons, the sauce is finished with a liaison of the blood of the animal in question.

Compôte. This term denotes a preparation of fresh or dried fruits, cooked in a syrup, which may be served hot or cold. The word "compôte" is also used for certain dishes featuring pigeon or partridge.

Consommé. An enriched clarified stock, prepared from meat, poultry or game, which is served as a clear soup. A fish consommé may also be featured on menus, i.e. "Consommé Nelson".

Couronne. Couronne means a crown. It is used to describe a dish which resembles a crown. An example of this is "Couronne d'agneau" which is prepared by placing two raw best ends of lamb back to back and securing them with string. When the joint is cooked it is often garnished with bouquets of vegetables.

Crème. A term which may be applied to whipped cream, butter and custard creams used to garnish pastries and cakes. It also describes soups, egg custard, sauces and sweets. Many dishes are termed "à la crème" meaning that a quantity of cream has been used in the preparation, i.e. "Escalope de veau à la crème".

Cromesquis. A preparation consisting of chicken or beef, bound in a thick sauce, i.e. a "velouté", thickened with yolks of eggs. When the mixture is cold it is formed into croquettes, wrapped in a pig's caul, dipped in frying batter and deep-fried.

Croquembouche. Also written as "croque-en-bouche", may refer to all kinds of sweet preparations which easily crunch and crumble in the mouth; this is the literal meaning of the term.

5

The typical "Croquembouche" consists of "profiteroles" glazed with sugar, which has been cooked to 315°F, i.e. "crack" stage. Croquembouche may also be made from nougat, iced cakes and fruits all dipped in boiled sugar.

Croustade. A description applied to various dishes, which usually consist of puff-pastry cases, although sometimes pieces of bread hollowed out and fried are used; filled with various savoury preparations.

Croûtes. These are made from various types of bread or "brioche" and featured in the preparation of hors d'œuvre, entrées and sweets or as a garnish for soups. If they are to be used as a garnish for soups they are prepared from bread and are usually known as "croûtons". An example of a sweet using a "croûte", which in this case consists of a stale savarin, is "Croûte aux fruits". The word "croûte" is also used to describe certain savouries, i.e. "Croûte Derby".

Currie or **Kari.** A "ragoût" flavoured with curry powder, mainly applicable to chicken, lamb or beef, although sometimes a prawn or shrimp curry may be featured on a menu. A chicken curry is written as "Currie de volaille". Curry powder is made by combining various spices which include cardamon seed, coriander seed, cummin seed, turmeric, pepper, cinnamon, mace, bayleaves, cloves and saffron. The strength of a curry depends to a large extent upon the amount of chillies included in the particular curry powder; it owes its colour and smell to the presence of turmeric. Curry is derived from the Hindu "Khura" meaning palatable.

Darne. A term which is used to describe a slice of a large round fish such as salmon or cod. The slices are taken from the middle of the fish and are cooked on the bone in various ways, i.e. braised, poached, grilled or shallow fried.

Délice. This word implies delectability, but because of its vagueness is often misused. It is sometimes used as a substitute for the word fillet, as in the term "délice de sole".

Demi-glace. Half-glaze. A sauce which is the basis of many sauces used in the kitchen. It is made from a refined "Espagnole" sauce and finished with sherry. "Espagnole" sauce is prepared from a brown "roux" to which is added brown beef stock, tomato purée or fresh tomatoes and a "mirepoix" (explained on p. 11.) for flavouring.

Diablotins. These are round slices of French bread cut ⅓ inch thick, covered with a thick "béchamel" sauce, which is strongly flavoured with cheese and cayenne pepper. They are sprinkled with grated Parmesan cheese and browned under the salamander. "Diablotins" are served with vegetable "purée" soups which are known as "Garbure", of which there are several varieties.

Écrevisse. Crayfish, which are like miniature lobsters in appearance, live entirely in fresh water and are considered a great delicacy. They are used for a soup, i.e. "Bisque d'écrevisse", garnishes and many other dishes.

Émincé. This means finely sliced or shredded. It is also a name of a dish utilizing cooked meat or poultry, i.e. "Émincé de volaille". Various sauces may be used in the preparation of an "émincé", such as "chasseur", "bordelaise", "piquante", "poivrade" or "Robert".

Entrecôte. Literally this term means "between the ribs" and is used for a steak cut between two ribs of beef, e.g. Wing Rib. Nowadays "entrecôtes" are cut from a boned sirloin. An "entrecôte minute" is an "entrecôte" which has been batted out thinly.

Epigramme. When used in the culinary sense this term refers to small fillets of poultry and game, and breast of lamb or mutton prepared as "entrées".

Filet. Fillet, which is the undercut of a loin of beef, mutton, veal, pork and game. The word "filet" also applies to boned breasts of poultry and the boned sides of fish.

Fleurons. These are small baked crescent shapes of puff pastry which are used for garnishing. Fish dishes are often garnished with "fleurons", a notable example being "filet de sole au vin blanc".

Fricassée. A white stew of chicken, rabbit or veal. A feature of the preparation of this dish is that the meat is first "stiffened" in butter without colour, then a sauce is prepared around the

7

meat. A garnish, if employed, is cooked with the meat; it is added to the dish when the meat is three-quarters cooked.

Fritot. A type of fritter, in which small pieces of meat and poultry are used; suitable items are collops of poultry, lamb or veal sweetbreads, calf's head and brains.

Galantine. A dish made from boned poultry or white meat, stuffed and pressed into a symmetrical shape. It is served cold and may be glazed with aspic jelly, or coated with "chaud-froid" sauce and decorated. It is suggested by some authorities that the term "galantine" derives from the old French word "galiné", meaning chicken.

Garniture. It means the garnishing of a dish with edibles of ornamental appearance. "Garni" denotes garnished, filled, or stuffed.

Gâteau. A round, square or oval-shaped flat cake, which is usually decorated.

Gigôt. A term which applies to a leg of lamb or mutton. "Gigôt d'agneau rôti"—Roast leg of lamb.

Gnocchi (Italian) (French—*Gnokis*). There are three types of mixture used in the preparation of "gnocchi".

1. The mixture is made by cooking semolina in milk, to which is then added, whilst hot, egg yolks, cheese, butter and seasoning. The preparation is then spread on a greased tray; when cool it is cut into various shapes. These are known as "gnocchi romaine" which when served as a farinaceous dish are sprinkled with parmesan cheese, melted butter and browned under the salamander, or in the oven. Nowadays they are usually finished with a cordon of tomato sauce.

2. This variety have a basis of "choux paste" to which cheese is added. The paste is piped in ½-inch lengths, using a piping bag and ½-inch plain tube, into simmering salt water; poached for approximately 10 minutes and drained well. These may be used as part of the garnish for "goulash" or served as a farinaceous course under the name of "gnocchi parisienne". The procedure adopted for the latter is as previously described except that they are bound in a thin "béchamel" sauce, placed in an earthenware dish, sprinkled

with cheese and browned under the salamander. "Gnocchi au gratin" are prepared in the same manner as "parisienne" substituting "mornay" sauce for "béchamel". "Gnocchi pascale" differs in that the gnocchi are cooked in a veal gravy, they may then be gratinated.

3. Potatoes are the principal ingredient of this type, usually "known" as "Gnocchi de pommes de terre" or "Gnocchi piémontaise". The potatoes are baked in their jackets, the pulp is scooped out and mixed whilst still hot with flour, butter, eggs and seasoning. This preparation is divided into balls the size of walnuts, these are pressed slightly, then poached for approximately 15 minutes. They are drained well, arranged in an earthenware dish, sprinkled with cheese and melted butter and gratinated; they may also be bound in a sauce, i.e. tomato sauce.

Goujon. Gudgeon. It is also a culinary term meaning small strips of various fish cut about 3 inches long and ½ inch wide, which are cooked in various ways.

Grenadins. These are small slices of veal cut from the leg or saddle, which are larded (explained on p. 10) and braised.

Grenouille. An edible frog. These frogs are eaten mainly in France and southern Germany; the hind legs are considered a great delicacy, the flavour of which is not unlike that of a young rabbit.

Hachis. Hash. The term derives from "hâcher", to chop. It applies mainly to a method of preparing fresh or cooked meat. In the case of cooked meat, this is usually bound with half-glaze sauce or tomato sauce and veal gravy. Other ingredients may be added, for example, a dice of potatoes, tossed in butter, for a dish known as "Hachis de bœuf américaine".[1]

Haricot. Bean. The name is also applied to a stew of mutton, garnished with haricot beans, i.e. "Haricot de mouton".

Jarret. Shin or knuckle. The term is used to describe a knuckle of veal—"jarret de veau"—which is used for stocks and stews, i.e. "Osso bucco" (explained on p. 12).

Kromeskis. A Polish word which has the same meaning as

[1] Escoffier, A., *Guide to Modern Cookery*, Heinemann, London.

9

croquette in French. The information given previously for "Cromesquis" (explained on p. 5), is also applicable to "Kromeskis".

Laitance. The soft roe of a fish; those from herring, carp or mackerel are considered as a delicacy. Herring roe is the most used, notably as a garnish for fish dishes, i.e. "belle meunière". They may also be served as a savoury.

Langues de chat. These are very small tea or dessert biscuits. Literally, the term means "cats' tongues" and may be used to describe fine wafers of chocolate.

Lardons. Lardons are strips of larding fat of varying lengths and thickness, threaded into meat, poultry and game by means of a larding needle. The word "lardon" is also used of coarsely or finely diced bacon, blanched and fried, which is added to certain dishes and garnishes.

Lazanges. An Italian word, which is used to describe strips of "nouille" paste, cut in the shape of wide ribbons. These are cooked in the same way as macaroni.

Lié. "Lié" means thickened or bound. It applies to creams, soups and sauces, i.e. thickened gravy—"jus lié".

Longe. Loin. The back portion nearest the leg of an animal, loin of veal—"longe de veau".

Lorgnette. This name applies to fried onion rings, also to small dessert biscuits or candied fruits. The word "lorgnette" is also French for opera glasses and is used to describe a method of preparing whiting. The backbone of the fish is removed and both fillets are curled and placed in its mouth. The fish is then passed through flour, egg and breadcrumbs and deep fried, i.e. "merlan en lorgnette".

Macaroons. These are small, dry, round pastries made of almonds, sugar and the white of eggs. The macaroons of Nancy, which have a reputation dating back to the seventeenth century, are considered the best. The origin of macaroons is unknown, the French for macaroon is "macaron".

Macédoine. A mixture of raw or cooked fruits or vegetables, which may be served hot or cold. Carrots and turnips when used for a "macédoine" are usually cut in $\frac{1}{4}$-inch dice. The name "macédoine" derives from Macedonia, the country formed by small States which were conquered by Alexander the Great.

Matelote. A rich brown fish stew prepared mainly from freshwater fish such as carp, tench or pike; red or white wine may be used in this dish. A "matelote à la normande", however, is made from sea fish, mainly sole, conger eel and gurnet, cider is used instead of wine.

Médaillion. Medallion. A name which is given to round fillets, also to meat and other preparations which are shaped in a round form.

Mignon. A term which applies to the point or thin end of a whole fillet of beef, also to whole fillets taken from lamb, i.e. "filet mignon".

Mirepoix. A culinary term which describes a mixture of roughly cut carrots and onions, and in certain cases bacon, bayleaf and thyme. The vegetables and bacon are usually fried or tossed in butter before being added to soups and sauces as flavouring. Origin: Chapter 4, p. 63.

Miroton. A type of stew made from cooked meat, flavoured with onions. Some authorities suggest that this dish was known as "Mironton" in the eighteenth century, taken from the nursery rhyme "Marlborough-s-en-va-t-en guerre", which has the refrain, "Mironton-Mironton-mirontaine", and that later it became corrupted to "Miroton".

Navarin. A brown stew of lamb or mutton which is garnished with button onions and potatoes. A "navarin printanier" is garnished with Spring carrots and turnips, button onions, new potatoes, green peas, and french beans, cut into lozenges. The name is of ancient origin, being mentioned in one of the plays of Sodelle in the early seventeenth century.

Noisette. Hazel-nut. It is also a culinary term for small pieces of meat taken from a loin of lamb, with the bone and the majority of fat removed. "Noisette" is sometimes used to describe small slices of a fillet of veal or beef.

Noix de veau. Cushion or nut of veal, which is used for escalopes, roasting, braising or "sauté".

Nouilles. Noodles. These are prepared from a paste, which is made from flour, eggs, olive-oil and salt. The paste is rolled out very thinly, cut into thin strips and cooked in the same way as macaroni, or in butter. Noodles are used for garnishing or served as a farinaceous dish.

Ognonnade or **oignonade.** A stew containing a large proportion of onions. The term also applies to finely chopped onion, melted in butter or cooked in white wine.

Ortolan. A small bird similar in size to a lark which enjoys a high reputation as a table delicacy. Ortolans are found in central and southern Europe, particularly at Landes in the south of France.

Osso Bucco (Italian). A type of stew utilizing slices from the middle part of a knuckle of veal. The slices are cut across the knuckle approximately $1\frac{1}{2}$ inch thick, resulting in a piece of meat surrounding a piece of bone. These slices are seasoned and shallow fried in butter and oil; finely chopped onions and "tomate concassée" are added, the meat is barely covered with a tomato flavoured "demi-glace" sauce and braised, the dish is finished with chopped parsley. A variation of this dish may be the addition of a "brunoise" or carrots, celery and leeks, with white wine included in the sauce prior to the braising. A mixture of finely chopped zest of orange, chopped garlic and parsley may be used to complete the dish. Often a "rizotto" containing saffron is served with "Osso Bucco".

Panada. A culinary term describing a preparation which may be used to bind the ingredients of a stuffing together. There are various types of panada, e.g. bread or flour panada,[1] varying according to its intended use and the forcemeat required; see "Quenelles", p. 14.

Pannequets. Pancakes. These may be sweet or savoury. "Pannequets" is derived from the English word "pancakes".

Parfait. A light ice which may be prepared from variously flavoured mixtures.

Pâté. A pie; pasty; a savoury meat preparation, or a raised pie.

Paupiette. An old French word which originally had the same

---

[1] Escoffier, Auguste, *Guide to Modern Cookery*, Heinemann, London.

meaning as "papillotte". It now means a thin slice of meat or poultry, which is stuffed, rolled up and tied with string, i.e. "Paupiette de bœuf".

Petits fours. This name is given to all kinds of very small fancy cakes, crystallized fruits and "bon-bons".

Piquante. "Piquante" means sharp of flavour or stimulating. This term describes a sharp sauce which has a "demi-glace" basis, to which has been added a reduction of vinegar, crushed peppercorns, shallots and sometimes white wine. This sauce when finished with chopped gherkins, parsley, chervil, and tarragon, is known as "sauce piquante".

Poivrade. Peppery, from the French "poivre" meaning pepper. It is also used to describe a method of preparing certain meats, especially ground game, in which a "sauce poivrade" is used.

Poularde. A fat pullet; a chicken about 7 or 8 months old that has not started to lay eggs. It is especially suitable for roasting and pot-roasting. The undrawn weight of an average "poularde" is between 4–6 lb.

Poulet de grain. A Spring chicken of about 3–4 months old, which usually weighs $1\frac{1}{2}$–2 lb (undrawn). These chickens are roasted, pot-roasted or grilled.

Poulet à la Reine. A name given to fine specimens of young chickens which have an undrawn weight of between 2–4 lb.

Poussin. Baby or Spring chicken which is from 4 to 6 weeks old. A single baby chicken usually weighs 12 oz–1 lb (undrawn) and a double baby chicken, "poussin double", weighs 1–$1\frac{1}{2}$ lb.

In addition to the above, a common hen, i.e. a bird which is past the period at which it is tender enough to be roasted is known as "une poule". This bird is suitable for boiling and may feature on a menu as "Poule au riz". In this case it is garnished with rice and served with a "sauce suprême".

Profiteroles. These are small balls of choux paste, piped through a piping bag on to a greased baking tin and baked. "Profiteroles" are of varying size depending upon their use. They may be filled with various fillings, for example, a purée of game or cheese and used for garnishing "consommé": in this case they are very small. Larger "profiteroles" are served as a

13

sweet and may be filled with fresh cream, pastry cream or jam. They are often served coated with a chocolate sauce and sprinkled with almonds, as "profiteroles au chocolat".

Purée. A word which denotes a smooth pulp or mashed vegetables. It is also used to describe thick soups.

Quenelles. These are made with a forcemeat, which can consist of fish, meat, game, poultry or crustaceans, bound with eggs and/or panada. The meat or fish which is to be made into "quenelles" is first pounded in a mortar, or, nowadays, finely minced two or three times and placed in a "bowl-chopping" machine. Some culinary writers suggest that the name derives from the Anglo-Saxon word "knyll", which meant to pound or grind. Quenelles may be large or small and shaped in various forms, they are served as "entrées" or used as a garnish for soups or "entrées". A fine chicken forcemeat or "mousseline" mixture may be used for quenelles; this mixture does not include a panada.[1]

Râble. A term which is used to describe the back or loin part of a rabbit or hare.

Ragoût. A rich, seasoned stew of meat. The meaning of the word "ragoût" is to "give again taste", which is achieved during the cooking process, by the combination of materials used.

Ramequins (Ramekins). These are small tarts or tartlets filled with a cream cheese. The term may also be applied to small pastries prepared from a cheese-flavoured choux pastry. Individual earthenware dishes are also known as ramekins.

Ravigote. A cold sauce which consists of a "vinaigrette", with the addition of chopped onions and capers, flavoured with chervil and tarragon. A sharp hot sauce prepared from a "velouté" and finished with herbs is also called "ravigote". The name of these sauces has been taken from the French verb "ravigoter" meaning to revive or reinvigorate.

Ravioli. These are very small squares or rounds of "nouille" paste enclosing a highly flavoured forcemeat. The most common filling consists of spinach, calves' brains, finely chopped or minced braised beef, bound with eggs and flavoured with

[1] Escoffier, Auguste, *Guide to Modern Cookery*, Heinemann, London.

herbs. Other forcemeats are prepared by substituting cooked chicken or chicken livers, or cheese for the braised beef. Ravioli are poached in salt water, drained, served in an earthenware dish, sprinkled with grated Parmesan cheese and served with various sauces.

Rissoles. These consist of a mixture prepared from fish or meat, which is enclosed in pastry, usually puff pastry. They are often shaped in half-moons, like a turnover and are fried in fat or butter.

Rouge de Rivière. A French name for the shoveller duck, a type of wild duck.

Roulade. A meat roll, rolled meat or small galantine.

Roux. A culinary term which applies to a mixture of cooked flour and fat, used to thicken sauces. The amount of flour required in proportion to the fat depends on the desired consistency of the sauce. The fat used is normally butter or margarine but in some sauces dripping or lard is substituted.

Royan. A delicately flavoured small fish, similar to a large sardine.

Ruban. Ribbon. "Rubané" means "ribbon-like"; an example of its application is a "bavarois rubané" which consists of different flavours of bavarian cream arranged in layers.

Salami. An Italian sausage, used chiefly for sandwiches and "hors d'œuvre".

Salpicon. A mixture of ingredients, which may be diced or sliced, and is sometimes blended with a sauce.

Schnitzel. A term much used in Germany and Austria to designate a thin slice of meat, chiefly veal. It is also used in this country in many restaurants to describe an escalope of veal, i.e. "Wiener Schnitzel".

Selle. Saddle, which consists of two loins undivided. Saddle of mutton—"selle de mouton".

Soufflé. A very light baked or steamed pudding; an omelet. The description also applies to light savoury creams.

Suprême. This means the best or most delicate. The term is used to describe a cut of poultry or game, i.e. "suprême de volaille"— wing and breast of chicken. It also applies to a cut of certain fish, for example, salmon.

Tagliarini. A paste, similar to that used for macaroni, cut in fine shreds.

Tagliati. "Nouille" paste cut in irregular, extremely thin pieces.

Talmouse. A sweet or savoury pastry, made in the shape of parson's caps.

Terrine. An earthenware dish in which meat, game and fish are cooked. The word "terrine" is also used to describe the food itself, i.e. "terrine de foie gras". (*Foie gras*—Fr. for goose liver.)

Timbale. Literally a "drinking cup". The term is now used to describe various types of metal, earthenware or china receptacles, in which food is cooked. The word "timbale" is also used to describe many preparations which are cooked or served in a pie crust.

Torte. An open tart baked in a round shallow tin, of which there are many varieties. "Torte" is a German word.

Tournedos. These are small slices taken from the heart of a fillet of beef. This cut is sautéed or grilled and garnished in various ways.

Tranche. A slice of meat, fish, melon, bread, pastry or cake, etc. "En tranche"—in slices.

Tronçon. This word refers to a slice of a flat fish, which includes the bone, for example, turbot—"tronçon de turbot".

Turban. A word which is used to describe the manner in which some foodstuffs are arranged in a circle on a dish. "Turban" also applies to dishes, mostly forcemeats of game, poultry or crustaceans which are cooked in border moulds, a reference to the head-dress worn in the East.

Tutti-frutti. An Italian expression for various kinds of fruits or a mixture of cooked vegetables. "Tutti-frutti" is also a name given to ice-cream preparations, mixed with different sorts of candied fruits.

Vacherin. A Jura cheese or an open cheese tart. It is more commonly known as a sweet, consisting of meringue piped in the form of a circle and cooked. This case is then filled with whipped cream and fruit, for example, raspberries.

Velouté. This word means smooth or "velvet-like". It describes a rich white sauce, made from a white stock, either chicken, veal or fish depending on its use, which is added to a white roux. When the sauce is thickened with egg yolks, flavoured with mushroom, liquor and lemon juice (then finished with cream) it is known as "sauce allemande". The term "velouté" is also used to describe certain thickened soups.

Vol-au-vent. A round or oval case made of puff-pastry which is filled, after cooking, with various kinds of mixtures bound with brown or white sauce. The fillings may consist of cooked meat, poultry, game, sweetbreads, fish or crustaceans.

Zabaglione. A frothing mixture consisting of yolks of eggs, sugar, wine and flavourings which is cooked while beating until it thickens. It is served hot or cold in glasses or used as an accompaniment to some hot sweets. The word "sabayon" in French is a corruption of the Italian word "zabaglione".

CHAPTER 3

Other Aspects of Menu Terminology

Cookery Processes and Styles of Preparation

This chapter is concerned with other aspects of menu terminology, involving the names of cooking processes, styles of preparation, countries of origin of dishes and geographical and regional associations. The purpose of this section is to examine these factors which have contributed greatly to the vast repertoire of classical dishes.

As many of the cooking processes and styles of preparation, in common use today, were developed by French chefs, it was only natural that the naming of them should be closely associated with the French language. There is, in some instances, a simple definition or translation, whereas others require a lengthy explanation. The language used, apart from indicating the method of cooking, also conveys to the knowledgeable which sauce or garnish is served with a particular dish.

Many dishes which have been named after their country of origin have been retained untouched thus adding to the international nature of the classical repertoire, whilst others have been modified or adapted by chefs, many of them French. Many countries have specialities which feature particular ingredients in several different dishes. In some cases a country is noted for the style of preparation of many of its dishes, or the method of cooking usually employed. An example of this is the English style of cooking which is expressed on menus as "à l'anglaise". This description denotes that the food is plainly cooked or that the dish is prepared in a manner typical of this country.

Another contributory element in the naming of dishes is that geographical associations exist with particular ingredients featured in them, or the use made of wines in their preparation. Many dishes are "named" because of these geographical associations, a good example being "Filet de bœuf périgueux"; a fillet of beef so described is served with a "sauce périgueux". This sauce and other dishes with the "périgueux" designation (see also *Périgourdine*, p. 47), include truffles and truffle essence (the sauce has a demi-glace base and is flavoured also with Madeira wine), owing to the especially good-quality truffles found in the Périgord district of France.

In this category also are regional dishes, of which I have included some of the most well known, as to list all of them would require a separate book.

Many names of towns or regions are adjectivalized and have become a part of menu language. These adjectives, expressing a style of preparation, are written in the feminine singular form owing to the fact that originally "à la française", for example, was written as "à la mode française". In most cases now, the "à la mode" is omitted, although the influence of the feminine singular noun "mode" still exerts itself on the grammatical form of the adjective. In some instances even the "à la" is not included, thus "petits pois à la française" becomes "petits pois française". In many instances where a place-name is adjectivalized there is often an indication that dishes prepared under this name have some common ingredients or style of preparation. This is often the case, but there are also numerous dishes where this does not apply as they do not conform to the expected pattern. I shall endeavour where possible to explain some of these irregularities, but there are some dishes for which I have been unable to find any explanation or relationship with other dishes although bearing the same name. It has been my intention to make this work as comprehensive as possible; however, I do not wish to imply that I have been able to define all the possible methods of preparing certain dishes, appearing under the various headings in this section.

Menu Terminology

Countries of Origin of Dishes, Geographical and Regional Associations

Africaine (à l'). African style, featuring North African products, particularly egg-plants, tomatoes, flap mushrooms which are usually cooked in oil.

Aillade. Applies to preparations which include garlic, an example is a "sauce aillade" which is a "vinaigrette" with garlic added.

Algérienne (à l'). Associated with Algeria. The name of a garnish applied principally to large pieces of meat, consisting of small tomatoes cooked in oil and sweet potato croquettes, or sweet potatoes cooked in butter.

Allemande (à l'). German style. This definition applies to dishes which are prepared in a manner peculiar to Germany. A dish garnished with sauerkraut and pork may be termed "à l'allemande" or dishes featuring smoked sausages may be similarly defined. A garnish "allemande" may also consist of noodles tossed in butter and mashed potatoes.

Alsacienne (à l'). From the French province of Alsace reputed for its foie-gras, sauerkraut, ham and many varieties of sausages. Thus, dishes with this designation usually feature some of these specialities as the predominating ingredients.

Ambassadrice. A method of preparing fish particularly fillets of sole; these are rolled round stuffed crayfish, poached, dressed in a timbale and coated with "Sauce normande". (This sauce has a basis of fish "velouté" flavoured with mushroom essence and juice of oysters. It is thickened with a leason of yolks of eggs and cream and finished with butter and cream.)

The term "ambassadrice" also denotes a method of preparing "tournedos" and "noisettes". These are "sautéed" in butter; garnished with mushrooms, chicken livers, cock's combs, and kidneys, braised lettuce and "noisette" potatoes. A thickened gravy flavoured with Madeira is served with this dish.

Américaine (à l'). A name given to various methods of preparation of fish, meat, eggs and vegetables which usually include tomatoes and in some cases bacon and red peppers. Among these preparations the best known is "Homard à l'américaine". The sauce which is made when preparing a lobster in this manner is known as "sauce américaine". There are many experts who assert that this method of cooking lobster originated in Brittany, and that the name "à l'américaine" is an error of transcription, the proper form being "à l'amoricaine".

Amiral (à l'). This description which signifies Admiral style is given to fish dishes. A characteristic feature of them is the garnish employed, which is composed of oysters, mussels, truffles, mushrooms and sometimes crayfish tails.

Ancienne (à l'). This means old fashioned or prepared in the old style. The garnish "ancienne" consists of kidney beans, hard-boiled eggs and braised lettuce, unless it is served with poultry or a "fricassée à l'ancienne" in which case it is comprised of button onions and button mushrooms.

Andalouse (à l'). Andalusian style. Preparations under this heading are characterized mainly by tomatoes, pimentoes, egg plants and a rice pilaff. A "sauce andalouse" is a mayonnaise sauce flavoured with tomato and garnished with a dice of sweet pimento.

Anglaise (à l'). English style. "A l'anglaise" usually implies that the method of preparing the food is plain, either boiled in water, or roasted, or that the dish is prepared in a manner typical of this country.

Anversoise (à l'). A garnish applicable to large and small cuts of meat, calves' sweetbreads and eggs, the main feature of which is hop shoots, cooked in butter or cream. The name derives from Antwerp.

Archiduc (à l'). A description which applies to a number of preparations, in particular to chicken and egg dishes. A feature of them is that they are usually seasoned with paprika pepper and blended with cream.

Ardennaise (à l'). From Ardennes. A term applying mostly to dishes of small birds, for example larks or thrushes, cooked in a "cocotte" with juniper berries.

Argenteuil. The name of a district in France which is renowned for its asparagus, therefore dishes with the "Argenteuil" designation feature asparagus. An example of this is a "potage Argenteuil".

Ariégoise (à l'). Associated with the district of Ariége, in France, which is famous for its mineral waters, geese, pork, ham and sausages. Dishes styled "à l'ariégoise" usually include green cabbage, pickled pork and kidney beans in the garnish.

Arlésienne (à l'). The name is derived from the town of Arles, in the south of France, which is famous for the sausages and excellent oil produced there. The garnish, which is served principally with small cuts of meat (noisettes and tournedos), consists of egg-plant, fried in oil, fried onion rings and tomatoes cooked in oil.

Armagnac (à l'). A method of cooking in which Armagnac brandy is used, usually to prepare a sauce, i.e. "Suprême de bécasse à l'armagnac" (Bécasse—French for woodcock). Armagnac is a region in the old French province of Gascony, which is famous for the excellent brandies produced there.

Astrakhan. A Russian province. It is also the name of a caviare, the best of its kind, exported from there.

Athénienne (à l'). A name applying to various dishes, all of which are flavoured with lightly fried onion and are garnished with egg-plants, tomatoes and sweet pimentoes.

au; aux. with; i.e. with rice—"au riz"; "aux nouilles"—with noodles, "au beurre"—with butter, either cooked or tossed in butter to complete the cooking process.

au beurre noir. With black butter; it is used to complete dishes, for example, "Raie au beurre noir". In this dish the skate is cooked in a "court bouillon" drained well on a cloth, and finished with black butter, vinegar and capers.

au bleu. A method of cooking freshwater fish, particularly trout, i.e. "truite au bleu". The fish becomes a bluish colour owing to being cooked when absolutely fresh, in a "court bouillon" containing vinegar or white wine, thyme, bayleaf, carrots and onions cut in small rings, and seasoning. The fish is passed through vinegar prior to cooking and is taken to the restaurant in the special receptacle in which it is cooked. In many first-class hotels a tank is installed in which trout are kept especially for this dish.

au four. This means "baked" or cooked in the oven. Potatoes baked in their jackets are an example of the application of this term, i.e. "Pommes de terre au four".

au gratin. Refers to dishes which acquire a crisp golden brown crust, either in a hot oven or under the salamander. To assist in the formation of the crust, dishes prepared in this manner are sprinkled with bread-crumbs, or grated cheese (sometimes both), preferably Parmesan cheese and melted butter.

au jus. Dishes of meat which are served in their own juice or gravy are described in this fashion. The term "au jus" also applies to vegetables, eggs and farinaceous dishes which are finished with a cordon of gravy.

Aurore (à l'). A style of preparation applicable to eggs, poultry and sweetbreads, which features a "sauce aurore". This sauce is prepared by blending a "velouté" and a tomato sauce.

Autrichienne (à l'). A distinctive feature of dishes with this name is that they are seasoned with paprika pepper. Fennel, onion and sour cream are sometimes included.

Auvergnate. The name comes from the region of Auvergne, in France. This region is noted for the quality of its beef, lamb, mutton, pork and pork products. Choice dessert fruits, excellent chestnuts and walnuts are also grown there. Oxtail, i.e. "Queue de bœuf à l'auvergnate", is braised, and garnished with chestnuts, braised button onions and lardons.

Badoise. There are two garnishes served with dishes of this name, which derives from the German town of Baden. The first,

23

which is served with large joints of meat, is composed of braised red cabbage, lean bacon and mashed potatoes. The other, suitable for "tournedos" and "noisettes", consists of stoned cherries.

Barigoule. A French name for a mushroom, which in the south of France is also called "brigoule" or "bourigoule". "A la barigoule" is a description given to artichokes which are stuffed with mushrooms.

Bavarois. A Bavarian cream which is composed of a custard (made with yolks of eggs, sugar and milk), gelatine and whipped cream. Nowadays, the beaten whites of the eggs are usually added and various flavourings are used. It is not known whether this preparation actually originated in Bavaria, as its name would seem to imply. A "sauce bavaroise" is prepared as for a "sauce hollandaise" with the addition of horseradish, to the reduction, the sauce is flavoured with crayfish and garnished with a dice of crayfish tails.

Béarnaise. A "sauce béarnaise" is similar to a "sauce hollandaise" excepting that tarragon stalks are added to the reduction. The sauce is finished with chopped tarragon and chervil. According to some authors of culinary works this sauce originated in Béarn. Other authorities claim that this sauce was made for the first time in the Henry IV pavilion at Saint Germain-en-Laye, and that it was thus named in honour of Henry IV, who was born at Pau in the province of Béarn.

Berçy. A locality of Paris which is an entrepôt for wines, brandy and mineral waters. There are two sauces with the name "berçy" both of which feature white wine in the reduction; a white sauce served with fish, made from a fish "velouté" and finished with butter and chopped parsley; a brown sauce, consisting mainly of meat glaze, garnished with a small dice of bone marrow and chopped parsley, which is served with grilled meats.

Bergère. A shepherdess. Dishes with this designation, which applies mainly to egg dishes, include a small dice of cooked lamb or mutton in their garnish. Other dishes with the name "bergère" usually feature mushrooms in some form.

Bellevue (en). A popular title which is applied to cold dishes of poultry or game, masked with white "chaud-froid" sauce and garnished with truffles, tongue, tarragon leaves and chopped aspic jelly. A brown chaud-froid sauce is also used.

Berrichonne (à la). The name derives from the French province of Berry. A garnish with this name, applicable to large joints of meat, is composed of balls of braised cabbage, small braised onions, whole chestnuts and slices of bacon.

Bigarade. A bitter or sour orange—Seville orange. A method of serving duckling, i.e. "Caneton bigarade" which is garnished with sections of oranges and coated with a "sauce bigarade".

Bohémienne (à la). Bohemian style. A feature of dishes with this name is the inclusion of paprika pepper and sour cream.

Bolonaise. A description applied to a method of serving spaghetti. A "sauce bolonaise" comprises diced or minced beef, chopped onions bound with a thickened gravy or "demi-glace". Bolonaise, often mis-spelt "bolognaise", derives from Bologna, which is famous for its sausages, an Italian speciality principally manufactured there. (It.—Bolognese.)

Bonne-femme (à la). Housewife style. This name applies to a soup prepared from leeks and potatoes, i.e. "Potage bonne femme". Fish, coated with a white wine sauce, containing sliced mushrooms, chopped shallots, chopped parsley and glazed under the salamander is also described as "à la bonne femme". A baked apple is known as "Pomme bonne femme".

Bordelaise (à la). A term which applies to a number of different dishes. The most common feature a "sauce bordelaise", which is made with a reduction of Bordeaux wine (claret), chopped shallots, thyme, bayleaf and peppercorns. A "demi-glace" sauce is then added to the reduction. "Tournedos bordelaise" is an example of a dish of this kind. "Bordelaise" when applied to fish dishes usually means that a "mirepoix" is used during the preparation, and in some cases a "sauce bordelaise" is made using white wine. Bordelaise is also the name of a garnish consisting of potatoes and artichokes. An exception to the usual interpretation of "bordelaise" is a "caneton à la bordelaise". The duckling is stuffed with a

25

mixture of breadcrumbs, the chopped, fried liver of the duck, chopped parsley, stoned olives, chopped mushrooms, garlic, seasoning and egg. It is then roasted and served, accompanied only by roast gravy.

Bouillabaisse. A celebrated fish stew which is a national French dish. All along the Mediterranean coast, from Cap Cerbère to Menton, a great variety of bouillabaisses is prepared, but to the purists, the only authentic bouillabaisse is the one made in the region from Marseilles to Toulon.

The Marseilles bouillabaisse is prepared from the following fish: rascasse, chapon, saint-pierre, conger-eel, angler-fish, red mullet, rouquier, whiting, sea-perch, spiny-lobster, crabs and other shell-fish. The other ingredients for this dish are onions, tomatoes, garlic, thyme, bayleaf, fennel, parsley, saffron, dry orange peel, olive-oil, seasoning, water or fish stock. The soup is served in a deep round dish on slices of special bread known as "marette" in Marseilles.

Bouilli. Bouilli means boiled, from the verb "bouillir"—to boil. It is also used in France as an abbreviation for boiled beef.

Boulanger. Baker. Sliced potatoes, sliced onions arranged in layers and cooked in stock are known as "pommes boulangère". Joints of lamb with the description "boulangère" are garnished with potatoes cooked in this manner. It is said that this garnish originates from the time when bakers used to cook customer's own food after the baking of bread had been completed.

Boulonnaise. This comes from the French fishing port, Boulogne. A method of preparing mackerel, garnished with mussels, is known under this name.

Bouquetière (à la). The name of a garnish used for meat dishes. It is composed of various vegetables placed in bouquets around the dish.

Bourgeoise (à la). This term signifies a dish prepared in a simple, homely, but nevertheless tasty and wholesome manner. It applies mainly to large pieces of braised meat, which are garnished with carrots, button onions and lardons.

Bourguignonne (à la). Derives from Bourgogne—Burgundy, a region of France renowned for its wines and the excellence of its cuisine. Meat, eggs, fish and poultry may all be prepared "à la bourguignonne". A feature of these dishes is the use of red Burgundy in the preparation of the sauce. They are garnished with button onions, mushrooms and lardons, with the exception of fish dishes, in which case the bacon is omitted.

Brabançonne (à la). Associated with Brabant, a Belgian province. A garnish for large pieces of meat is composed of endives, potato croquettes and sometimes hop shoots cooked in butter or cream. Small cuts of meat "à la brabançonne" are garnished with potato croquettes and small tartlets, filled with brussels sprouts, coated with "sauce mornay" and glazed.

Braisé. Braisé is from the verb "braiser" meaning "to braise". Braising is a combination of roasting and stewing. It is a method of cooking in a tightly covered pan in a liquid, the amount of which varies according to the food which is being cooked. The liquid employed may be stock, thickened gravy, or "demi-glace". Most foods are placed on a bed of roots (thick slices of carrot and onion) and are flavoured with a faggot. Large and small cuts of meat which are to be braised, are shallow fried prior to cooking, in order to seal the pores of the meat, thus retaining the juices in the meat.

Bretonne (à la). The name comes from Bretagne, the French province of Brittany. Most dishes with this designation include a garnish of haricot beans, either whole or in a purée; cooked with tomatoes, garlic, chopped onions, chopped parsley and white wine. A thick soup which is prepared from a purée of haricot beans is known as "potage bretonne". An exception to the usual interpretation of the name is a "sauce bretonne", which is served with eggs or fish. This sauce is made from a "velouté" or a white wine sauce and is garnished with thin strips of leeks, carrots and celery.

Broche. This means "a spit" which is used for roasting before an open fire. Food which is cooked in this manner is described as "à la broche".

Brouillé. A word usually applied to eggs, which means scrambled, mixed or beaten.

Brunoise. This name is associated with the French district of Brunoy (Seine-et-Oise), which is celebrated for the growth of fine spring vegetables. Brunoise is a description given to vegetables which are cut into very small dice, i.e. $\frac{1}{16}$ inch (or $\frac{1}{8}$ inch for broths). This is used as a garnish for soups and other dishes. The word may also mean a type of soup or a mixture of vegetables.

Bruxelloise (à la). This derives from the town of Brussels. The garnish for large pieces of meat is typical of Belgian cookery and includes braised chicory, brussels sprouts and "pommes château".

Caen. A town in France famous for its tripe and other delicacies, described as "à la mode de Caen".

Café. Coffee. Flavoured with coffee—"au café" for example, "Bavarois au café".

Cancalaise (à la). A garnish composed of oysters and shrimps. Cancale is a small fishing port on the French coast of the English Channel which is renowned for its "blonde" plump oysters.

Cardinal (à la). This is the form which is normally used, but strictly, it should be written "au Cardinal". It applies to a garnish for fish dishes which consists of slices of lobster and slices of truffles. "Cardinal" is also the name of a sauce, prepared from lobsters, "béchamel" fish stock and truffle essence, the colour of which is symbolic of the red worn by cardinals.

Carpentras (à la). This style of preparation features truffle either as a flavouring or as a garnish. Carpentras is a district where truffles of excellent flavour and size grow particularly well.

Casserole. A copper stewpan, also a fire-proof earthenware dish with a lid. When the term "en casserole" is used, it sometimes indicates a shape of rice or duchesse potatoes, filled with different preparations, i.e. minced meat or game purée. It also applies to a method of cooking and serving in an earthenware dish, for example, "poulet en casserole".

Cassoulet. A stew which is a speciality of the Languedoc region, where it originated. A "cassoulet" is prepared from pork and mutton, with goose or duck and haricot beans. It is cooked in an earthenware utensil which used to be known as the "cassole d'Issel", from which it derives its name.

Castillane (à la). A garnish suitable for small pieces of butcher's meat which comprises "tomate concassée" cooked in oil, small potato croquettes, and fried onion rings. The name is from Castille, in Spain.

Catalane (à la). A method of preparing large pieces of butcher's meat, garnished with egg-plants, cooked in oil, and a pilaf of rice. The garnish served with small cuts of meat, however, consists of globe artichokes and grilled tomatoes. Catalane derives from Catalonia, in the Spanish province of Barcelona.

Cendre (la). Ashes or embers. The term "cuit sous la cendre" means, literally, "cooked under the ashes". A method of cooking a ham is described as "sous la cendre". The ham is first poached and trimmed of skin, it is then sprinkled with sugar and glazed. It is then enclosed in pastry and cooked in the oven. After cooking, a little sherry or port wine is added, through a prepared hole in the pastry. A ham cooked in this manner is often garnished with "gnocchi", spinach or a cheese soufflé.

Cévenole. A method of preparing lambs' or calves' sweetbreads; these are braised, garnished with braised button onions, glazed chestnuts and brown bread "croûtons". The sweetbreads are coated with the reduced braising liquor, i.e. "Ris de veau Cévenole".

Chambord (à la). A method of cooking fish, particularly carp, in a "court bouillon" with red wine. A sauce is prepared from the cooking liquor and the fish is garnished with white turned mushrooms, fish quenelles decorated with truffles, soft roes tossed in butter, crayfish tails and slices of truffles. The dish is named after the locality of Chambord, where the old residence of the Kings of France, the Château de la Loire, was situated.

Champagne. A province of France renowned for its great sparkling wines. Several dishes are prepared employing champagne in the cooking. An example of this is "filets de sole au champagne", in which the fillets are poached in champagne and the cooking liquor is used for the sauce.

Chantilly (à la). Associated with Chantilly, a town in the department of Oise. Dishes with this designation always include cream. A "crème Chantilly" is whipped double cream, sweetened and flavoured. A "sauce Chantilly" can be either a "hollandaise" or a "mayonnaise" sauce to which whipped cream has been added. These sauces are also known as "sauce mousseline".

Chasseur (à la). This term signifies hunter's style or dishes which may be prepared quickly, and applies to small cuts of meat (tournedos), poultry or eggs. The main characteristic of dishes prepared in this manner is a "sauce chasseur".

Chaud-froid. A name given to various dishes prepared from poultry, game, cutlets, etc., masked with a cold sauce and served cold, often garnished with truffles and masked with aspic jelly. It is said that the name "chaud-froid" was given to a chicken dish by the Maréchale de Luxembourg, who on returning to his castle at Montmorency, having been called away from a dinner, asked for a "fricassée de volaille", which had been on the menu, to be served cold to him. He is said to have been so pleased with this dish, that he later asked for it again and insisted that it should appear on the menu as "chaud-froid".

Chipolata (à la). A garnish, which applies to poultry and large pieces of meat, consisting of chipolata sausages, glazed button onions, whole chestnuts and lardons.

Clamart. A locality near Paris, famous for its garden produce, especially peas. A garnish "Clamart" always features peas in some form.

Cloche. A "cloche" is the name of a glass utensil which is used to cover certain items of food while cooking, for example mushrooms or wings of chicken. Mushrooms which are cooked in this manner would appear on a menu as "Champignons sous cloche".

Cockie-leekie. A clear soup in which leeks, fowls and prunes form the main ingredients. This soup is a favourite Scottish dish.

Cocotte. An earthenware or porcelain fireproof dish made in single portion size or larger. Chicken, eggs, etc., may be cooked "en cocotte"; they are usually served in the dish in which they are cooked.

Copeaux. This means "shavings". "Pommes en copeaux" are shavings of potatoes which are deep-fried.

Cousinette. A soup made with spinach, lettuce, sorrel and other green herbs all of which are cut up finely. This soup is a speciality of Béarnaise cookery.

Crapaudine (à la). A name for a preparation of fowl, particularly of pigeon. The birds are cut, flattened and spread in the shape of a toad, which is said to be the reason for this name, as the French for toad is "crapaud". "Poulet à la crapaudine" is prepared in this manner, grilled and garnished with sliced gherkins. A similar dish in English cookery is "Spatchcock", otherwise known as "Poulet grillé à l'anglaise". The chicken is cut in similar fashion to "crapaudine", the wings are fixed by means of a skewer, the chicken is seasoned, brushed with melted butter and half-cooked in the oven. It is then sprinkled with breadcrumbs and melted butter and the cooking completed by grilling. A garnish of gherkins surrounds the chicken which is often accompanied by "sauce diable".

Crème (à la). Numerous dishes are styled "à la crème", meaning that a quantity of cream or "sauce crème" has been incorporated either before or after they have been cooked.

Créole (à la). A name given to various preparations signifying "Créole-style". A distinctive feature of many of them is the inclusion of rice, often a rice pilaff, garnished with red peppers, tomatoes and mushrooms cooked in oil. "A la Créole" also applies to a number of sweet dishes, some of which contain rice and are flavoured with oranges. The term is also used to describe some sweets which are masked with chocolate.

Croûte (en). This means encrusted; wrapped or enclosed in a paste, prior to cooking. An example of the application of this term is a "filet de bœuf piqué en croûte".

Danoise (à la). Danish style, which usually signifies that fish is featured in some form.

Daube (en). A method of cooking meat. This term usually applies to beef, which is cut into 4-oz pieces. These are larded and then marinaded in red wine and vinegar with a little spice. The meat is braised with fresh bacon rind, cut into squares, button onions, carrots shaped like olives, celery, garlic and a faggot containing parsley stalks, thyme, bayleaf and dry lemon rind. This method of cooking is also applicable to poultry, game and other meats. A notable example is a "daube" prepared from mutton known as "Daube à l'Avignonnaise".

Dauphine (à la). A name which is given to several different dishes. It applies most commonly to a potato preparation, made from two-thirds "pomme duchesse" mixture and one-third "chou-paste". This mixture is formed into cork shapes or balls and deep-fried.

Dauphinoise (à la). This designation usually indicates a method of cooking potatoes. Gratin dishes of many kinds (macaroni, meat, potatoes, crayfish tails) are popular in the Dauphine region; this potato dish is one of the most famous. The potatoes are sliced thinly and cooked in milk with egg, grated gruyere cheese, seasoning and nutmeg, in an earthenware dish which is buttered and rubbed with garlic. This dish is cooked in the oven and the potatoes are served in the dish in which they are cooked.

Deauvillaise (à la). This title comes from Deauville, a fashionable French seaside resort. The name applies particularly to a method of preparing fish, for example sole. The fish is cooked in cream, with finely chopped onion, butter is added to the reduced cooking liquor to make a sauce. The dish is garnished with shapes of puff pastry.

Demi-deuil (en). This term literally means, in "half-mourning". It describes poultry, veal, or veal sweatbreads, which are larded with truffles. Poultry is poached whereas the sweetbreads are braised. Food cooked in this way is masked with a "sauce suprême" and garnished with truffles, which explains why these dishes are so called.

Diable (à la). Devilled, from "diable" meaning "devil". The term is used to describe a method of preparing grilled fish, meat or poultry, with the addition of very hot condiments and sometimes a highly seasoned sauce, i.e. "sauce Diable".

Dieppoise (à la). This title derives from the French port of Dieppe which is noted for shrimps. The garnish "Dieppoise" consists of shrimps, mussels, and white mushrooms and applies particularly to poached fillets of sole which are masked with a white wine sauce.

Dijonnaise (à la). This comes from Dijon, the capital of the ancient province of Burgundy. Dijon is particularly famous for its mustard. Other specialities include "tripe á la dijonnaise", gingerbread, "Jambon persillée", and snails. The snails of Burgundy are known throughout the world as being the most succulent. Two well-known methods of preparing them are "à la bourguignonne" and "à la dijonnaise".

Duchesse (à la). A name given to various preparations, especially a method of preparing potatoes, known as a Duchesse mixture. This consists of a purée of potatoes, blended with yolks of egg and butter. It is made into "pommes duchesse" which are also used as a garnish for large joints of meat, in which case they are piped in various shapes. The mixture is also used as a border for various dishes, especially fish and for savoury cases.

Écossaise (à la). Scottish style. One of the characteristic features of Scottish cookery is the use of barley, as in Scotch Broth and "Gigôt d'agneau à l'écossaise".

Égyptienne (à la). This derives from Egypt. A "purée égyptienne" is prepared from yellow split peas.

Espagnole (à la). Spanish style, which usually signifies that onions and tomatoes are included in some form, i.e. "omelette espagnole". "Espagnole" is also the name of a rich brown sauce, the foundation of "demi-glace" and most brown sauces.

Étouffé (à la). A method of cooking food in a tightly closed vessel with very little liquid, or even without liquid. This method of cooking is also called "à l'étuvé" and is suitable for all kinds of good-quality meats, poultry, and vegetables to which a suitable amount of butter or oil is added. Fruit may also be cooked "à l'étouffé".

Farci. Farci means stuffed. The word "farce" derives from the Latin word "farcire" to fill or to stuff.

Fécampoise (à la). This comes from Fécamp, a French seaport. "Sole à la fécampoise" is poached, garnished with mussels and shrimps. A shrimp sauce is masked over the fillets of fish and the garnish. "Fleurons" are placed around the dish.

Fermière (à la). Farmer's style. A feature of dishes with this name is the inclusion of vegetables in the garnish, i.e. carrots, turnips, onions and celery, usually cut in "paysanne". Large joints of meat or poultry are often prepared in this fashion, either braised or "poëlé". A soup and a fish dish are also known under this heading.

Financière (à la). This term relates to preparations which are rich in expensive ingredients. It applies to meat and poultry which are garnished with sliced cock's combs, cock's kidneys, mushrooms, slices of truffles, stoned olives and very small chicken quenelles, bound with a Madeira sauce. Sweetbreads and calf's head are also prepared "à la financière". Sweetbreads with the garnish "financière" are often served in "vol-au-vent" cases or "croustades".

Fines herbes. A combination of finely chopped herbs, parsley, tarragon and chervil, mostly used in omelettes, salads and sauces. An omelette prepared in this way would appear on a menu as "Omelette aux fines herbes".

Flamande (à la). Flemish style. A name given to a garnish for large pieces of meat which is composed of small balls of braised cabbage, turned carrots and turnips, diced belly of pork and boiled potatoes. A feature of this style when applied to soups and egg dishes is the inclusion of brussels sprouts, usually in a purée, and potatoes.

Exceptions to the usual interpretation of "à la flamande" are: Asparagus "à la flamande", which is served hot with melted butter and halves of boiled eggs: and "carbonnade" which is made with slices of beef, cooked in beer with slices of onions

Florentine (à la). This derives from Florence. Italian cooks popularized the use of spinach in France. This title, which is applicable to numerous dishes of eggs, fish, meats and poultry always means that they are garnished with spinach.

Forestière (à la). A feature of this style of preparation when applied to meats and poultry is the inclusion in the garnish of mushrooms, flap mushrooms or morels, bacon and shallow fried potatoes, either "Parmentier" or "cocotte". A "crème forestière" is a cream of mushroom soup garnished with a "julienne" of mushrooms.

Française (à la). French style. This designation applies to numerous dishes, generally of French origin. The term cannot be said to mean anything in particular, as it is used to describe many simple preparations as well as those which are quite elaborate. Apart from variations in methods of preparations, the garnish varies in almost every case.

Frappé. Meaning iced or chilled. It is used to describe such items as melon.

Frit or **Frite.** This means fried, from the verb "frire", to fry. Frying is a cooking process by which articles of food are cooked, by being immersed in hot fat or oil.

Fumé. This applies to ham, bacon and various fish which are smoked. Salmon and trout are well known for their delicacy after being smoked.

Gastronome. This title suggests worthy of exalted taste or excellent preparation. A garnish with this name is applicable to poultry or veal sweetbreads, and consists of chestnuts, small truffles, small morels and cock's kidneys.

Gauloise (à la). This comes from Gaul. This name applies particularly to a clear chicken soup, thickened with yolks of eggs or tapioca. It is garnished with cock's combs and kidneys, slices of ham forcemeat or ham "royale".

Génevoise (à la). Derives from "Genève", Geneva. A "sauce génevoise" is a rich brown fish sauce, flavoured with red wine, which is served with salmon or salmon trout. This sauce was formerly called "sauce génoise".

Génoise (à la). Genoese style. A "sauce génoise" is a mayonnaise

35

flavoured with herbs with the addition of a purée of almonds and pistachio nuts.

Glacé. Glacé means glazed or iced. The term is used to describe a method of cooking vegetables, e.g. carrots, "carottes glacées". These may be shaped as olives or small barrels or cut into a regular size; they are placed in a pan, preferably with sloping sides, barely covered with water, salt, sugar and butter are then added. The pan is covered with greased grease-proof paper and a lid and the vegetables set to cook. When these are almost cooked the paper and lid are removed and the remaining liquor reduced over a fairly fierce heat until a glaze is formed around the vegetables, which must be tossed frequently during the process, hence the advantage of a sloping sided pan.

Grandmère (à la). This designation implies that the preparation is old fashioned, literally translated it means "grandmother's style". A garnish of mushrooms and "croûtons" is served with such dishes as "poulet en cocotte grandmère". In some establishments lardons and "pommes cocotte" are added to the garnish. Other dishes, for example pork chops and "hachis", are prepared "à la grandmère" but do not have the above garnish.

Grecque (à la). Strictly speaking, dishes "à la grecque" should be of Greek origin. There are some dishes which are described as "à la grecque" which are in fact of French origin. Among dishes with this name are vegetables, for example artichokes, leeks, cauliflowers and onions which are prepared as "hors d'œuvre". Rice is often featured in dishes with this designation.

Grillé. Means grilled. This is a method of cooking on greased grill bars with the aid of fat, over direct heat. In former times, grilling was accomplished over an open wood fire or charcoal. Nowadays, grill bars are heated by gas, electricity, coke and sometimes charcoal. Grilling, or broiling, is also achieved on modern appliances; under heat, i.e. salamander; between heat, i.e. between electrically heated grill bars. Only first-class cuts of meat or poultry and certain fish are suitable for grilling.

Haggis. A dish which may be regarded as the national dish of Scotland. A haggis consists of the heart, liver and lungs of a sheep par-boiled in salt water. These are finely chopped or minced and mixed with onions, oatmeal, beef suet, seasoning, nutmeg, lemon juice and a little gravy or stock. This mixture is placed into the sheep's stomach which has been thoroughly cleaned and turned inside out. The paunch is filled just over half-way, leaving plenty of space at the top to prevent it from bursting during the cooking. It is advisable to wrap it in a cloth in case it should still burst, while it is poached for 3–4 hours. Haggis is served on a well-starched folded napkin on a flat round dish. Whisky is the traditional drink which accompanies it; a purée of turnips is often served, or "mashed neeps and chappit tatties".

Hochepot. Hotch-potch. The name of a soup or type of stew which is very popular in Scotland. It is usually made from neck of mutton and beef with various vegetables, peas or barley and beans. It is therefore a mixture of food, hence its name. A broth prepared in France, known as "Hochepot", is composed of pig's ears and tails, breast of beef, breast and shoulder of mutton, bacon and a mixture of vegetables. Oxtail may also be prepared "en hochepot". The oxtails are braised with pig's trotters and pig's ears, and garnished with cabbage, carrots, turnips, small onions and chipolata sausages.

Hollandaise. This signifies Dutch style, which usually means that eggs are featured. A "sauce hollandaise" is a "warm" sauce made from a reduction of peppercorns and vinegar with yolks of eggs (cooked to a sabayon) and melted butter. This sauce is served with egg dishes; poached fish, i.e. salmon or turbot, and vegetables; cauliflower, asparagus or artichokes.

Hongroise (à l'). Hungarian style. A distinctive feature of dishes prepared "à l'hongroise" is that they are seasoned with paprika pepper and invariably contain cream in the sauce. This method of preparation is applicable to meats, poultry, fish, eggs and potatoes. Among these dishes probably the most well known is a stew prepared from veal or beef known

37

as a "goulash". Several kinds of goulash are prepared in Hungary, one of which is a "goulash" soup.

Indienne (à l'). Indian style. This description usually applies to dishes which contain curry powder or chutney and rice.

Irish stew. A stew, comprised mainly of mutton, onions and potatoes, which is a national dish of Ireland.

Irlandaise (à l'). Irish style. This term is applied to dishes which contain potatoes, either added during the cooking process or served around the dish as a garnish.

Italienne (à l'). A name given to various dishes prepared from poultry, fish, meat and vegetables. Many of these dishes include finely chopped or diced mushrooms or a "sauce italienne". "Noisettes", "tournedos" or "suprême de volaille" are garnished with quarters of artichokes and masked with a "sauce italienne". The garnish for large joints of meat is composed of quarters of artichokes and croquettes of macaroni. A method of preparing macaroni or other pasta with butter and Parmesan cheese is also known as "à l'italienne".

Japonaise (à la). A number of different dishes are called "à la japonaise". Most of them have this in common, that stachys, known also as Chinese artichokes, are included in the ingredients. Stachys are the tubers of a plant originating in China or Japan. They were cultivated in France for the first time at Crosnes; in French they are called "Crosnes de Japon". The garnish for large joints of meat consists of Chinese artichokes, tossed in butter, placed in "croustades" and "pommes croquettes". "Salade Francillon" is sometimes called "Salade à la japonaise". It is made from mussels, potatoes and truffles. There are three other salads known as "japonaise". Oysters, herrings and potatoes are the main ingredients of one, whereas the others feature fruit. The term "japonaise" is also applied to an iced "bombe" made of peach ice-cream filled with tea-flavoured mousse.

Jardinière (à la). A garnish, which as its name implies, consists of a mixture of spring vegetables, i.e. carrots, turnips, peas, small kidney beans, French beans cut into lozenges and small buds of cauliflowers. This garnish is served with roast, stewed or braised meats and pot-roasted poultry. The term "jardin-ière" is also used to describe vegetables which are cut into batons, approximately ¾ × ⅛ × ⅛ inch.

Juive (à la). Jewish style. One of the main features of Jewish cookery is the use of oil, especially for the frying of fish, i.e. "Truite à la juive". Sauce tartare is served separately.

Kaltschale. A fruit salad to which is added a liberal quantity of liqueur or wine. A dish which is popular in Russia.

Kebab. A name used in Turkey for various dishes in which skew-ered meat is featured. In this country the term usually des-cribes a dish of lamb, which consists of prime cuts of lamb, mushrooms and bayleaves, arranged on a skewer and grilled. This is known as "Kebab à la turque" and is usually served on a bed of rice pilaff.

Kedgeree. An Indian dish of curried fish and rice, which is often served as a breakfast dish in this country.

Languedocienne (à la). This name comes from the region of Languedoc, renowned for its foie-gras and truffles. Among the many specialities of this region is the famous "cassoulet de castelnaudray". The garnish served with "entrées à la languedocienne" consists of "tomates concassée", fried rings of egg-plants and sliced flap mushrooms tossed in oil. Sauces which are prepared for dishes of this sort are flavoured with garlic.

Liégeoise (à la). This comes from the Belgian town of Liége, near the Ardennes mountains. A characteristic feature of this method of cooking various foodstuffs is the use of juniper flavouring, i.e. thrush cooked in this manner, "Grives à la liégeoise". Juniper berries (*genièvre*) are the berries of a bush which grows wild in woods and mountain gullies; they are also used in the distillation of gin.

Limousine (à la). This designation derives from Limoges, a town in the old French province of Limousin. This area is noted for the excellence of the chestnuts, morels and flap mushrooms (*cêpes*) grown there. The term describes a method of cooking red cabbage in a buttered cocotte, with vinegar, a dice of

39

russet apples and pieces of cooked chestnuts. Cuts of meat and poultry, garnished with red cabbage, cooked in this way are called "à la limousine". Other dishes with this name include: a chicken stuffed with sausagemeat and mushrooms, which is garnished with chestnuts and lardons; brussels sprouts cooked, then tossed in butter with pieces of cooked chestnuts.

Lorraine. A district of high gastronomic repute, which has many specialities. One of the most famous is the "quiche lorraine", which is a flan with a filling, prepared from eggs, lean bacon, cream or milk.

Lyonnaise. Associated with Lyons in the Lyonnais region of France. There is an abundance of excellent onions in this district which are usually featured in dishes with this name, i.e. "tripe à la lyonnaise"; "sauce lyonnaise". Lyons sausage is a culinary speciality which is famous throughout the world.

Mâconnaise (à la). A name given to various meat dishes which are flavoured with red wine. Excellent wines are made from the grapes grown around the town of Mâcon, in the Saône-et-Loire department of France.

Madère (au). Flavoured with Madeira wine or featuring a "sauce Madère". This wine, which is made from grapes grown on the island of Madeira in the Atlantic Ocean, is one of the finest of fortified wines.

Madras. Generally applied to a dish flavoured with curry powder or chutney.

Madrilène (à la). Dishes with this designation, which comes from Madrid, are usually flavoured with tomato juice. A clear soup, often served cold, is known by this name, i.e. "Consommé madrilène".

Maître d'hôtel (à la). Hotel steward's fashion. This description usually applies to dishes which are quickly and plainly prepared, they usually feature parsley in some form. "Maître d'hôtel" is also the name of a flavouring butter, mixed with chopped parsley, lemon juice and seasoning. This butter is served with grilled meats and fish dishes.

Maltaise (à la). Maltese style. This term usually signifies that oranges are used, for example a "sauce maltaise" is a "sauce hollandaise" with the juice and zest of oranges added.

Maraîchère (à la). A method of preparation applied especially to large roast or braised cuts of meat, which are garnished with salsify, brussels sprouts and "pommes château". The name "maraîchère" actually relates to produce of the marsh but is extended to include garden produce.

Maréchale (à la). This term describes a method of preparing escalopes, wings of poultry and other small cuts of meat. Meat or poultry prepared in this way are dipped in egg and breadcrumbs and fried in butter, they are garnished with points of asparagus, and slices of truffles. In many establishments, "pommes parisienne" are added to the garnish. Another garnish with this name consists of small quenelles, slices of truffle and cock's combs.

Marocaine (à la). This derives from Morocco. This name usually refers to dishes which are cooked in oil and flavoured with garlic. A garnish "marocaine" includes tomatoes, "courgettes", gumbos and onions. An example of a dish prepared in this manner is a "Poulet sauté à la marocaine". However, "Sole à la marocaine" is garnished with a purée of sweet potatoes.

Marsala (au). Flavoured with marsala, a wine which in some respects resembles sherry of Madeira. Marsala wine is named after the town of Marsala in Sicily, near which the grapes are grown. "Piccata au marsala" is an example of the use of this wine. In this dish, very small escalopes of veal are cooked in butter in a sauté pan. The pieces of meat are placed on a dish, the pan is swilled out with Marsala and the resulting juices are poured over the meat.

Marseillaise. This comes from Marseille, a town in the south of France. Tomatoes, olives, oil, garlic, saffron and pimentoes are usually featured in dishes with this name. The garnish for small cuts of meat consists of tomatoes, filled with olives wrapped in anchovy fillets, cooked in oil and flavoured with garlic. "Pommes copeaux" are also included.

Matignon. A preparation of vegetables which is used as a garnish

41

for a number of dishes. The vegetables (carrots, celery and onions) are stewed in butter, flavoured with thyme, bayleaf and Madeira wine. Origin "Matignon" (Chap. 4).

Mentonnaise (à la). This derives from the town of Menton. It describes a method of cooking applicable to various foodstuffs especially rock-pool fish, in which the characteristic ingredients are tomatoes, black olives and garlic seasoning. It is also the name of a garnish consisting of small artichokes, stuffed baby marrows (courgettes) and small "pommes rissolécs".

Meunière (à la). Literally this term means "in the style of a miller's wife". It describes a method of cooking which mainly applies to fish. Fish cooked "à la meunière" is seasoned, lightly floured (which is believed to be the reason for the name "meunière") and shallow fried in clarified butter or oil. The fish is served on an oval silver flat dish, sprinkled with lemon juice, garnished with a slice of lemon and finished with "beurre noisette" and chopped parsley. Vegetables, for example chicory, are also prepared "meunière". The chicory is cooked "à l'étuvée" with butter and lemon juice, drained well, fried in butter and finished with lemon juice, "beurre noisette" and chopped parsley.

Mexicaine (à la). Mexican style. Pimentoes, tomatoes and mushrooms are usually featured in dishes with this designation. The garnish for large joints also includes egg-plants.

Milanaise (à la). This derives from the Italian town of Milan. Food which is prepared in this manner, i.e. escalopes of veal or lamb cutlets, is dipped in egg and breadcrumbs and shallow fried. It is garnished with spaghetti, bound in a tomato sauce with cheese, and a "julienne" of ham, tongue, mushrooms and truffles. Spaghetti or other pasta prepared in this manner is also served as a farinaceous dish.

Minestra. An Italian word for a thick soup. The best known soup of this kind is a "potage minestrone".

Minute (à la). A name given to dishes which may be quickly prepared, i.e. "Sauté de bœuf à la minute". This dish is made from thin strips or slices from the point of a fillet of beef, or point end of sirloin. Various sauces may be used, i.e. "chasseur, bourguignonne or bordelaise".

Mode (à la). This name is usually given to large joints of braised beef. Part of the rump is often used for this purpose. The piece is larded, marinaded in red wine for 6 hours, then braised with the addition of calves' feet. It is garnished with carrots, shaped like olives, button onions and the calves' feet cut in squares. "Bœuf à la mode" may be served hot or cold.

Moderne. A garnish for large joints of meat composed of stuffed tomatoes; bouquets of cauliflower, coated with mornay sauce and glazed; "pommes duchesse".

Mollet. Mollet means soft. "Œufs mollets"—soft-boiled eggs.

Monégasque (à la). This comes from Monaco. There are various dishes with the names of Monaco or Monégasque which have very varied ingredients. I have not been able to find any significant factor, apart from the inclusion of truffles or tomatoes in some of them.

Monte Carlo. This title usually indicates that tomatoes are featured. "Poulet Monte Carlo" was created by Escoffier when he was Chef at the Grand Hotel, Monte Carlo. Two methods of preparing sole with the name Monte Carlo are exceptions as they do not include tomatoes.

Montmorency (à la). Various dishes, cakes or sweets are given this name, usually signifying that cherries are included in one form or another, i.e. "caneton à la montmorency" or "gâteau montmorency". A variety of cherries cultivated at Montmorency take the name of this locality. "Filets de sole à la montmorency" is an exception to the usual interpretation of dishes with this name. A garnish served with tournedos consists of globe artichokes filled with balls of carrot and "pommes noisettes".

Montreuil. Most sweets which have this name include fruit in some form. One which is appropriately named is a "Charlotte Montreuil". A charlotte mould is lined with finger biscuits, it is filled with a "bavarois" containing peach purée and diced peaches. The peaches of Montreuil, which is in the neighbourhood of Paris, are well known for their excellence. A garnish

"Montreuil" served with tournedos consists of artichokes, filled with balls of carrot and peas.

Moscovien or **Moscovite.** Moscow style. Cold "moscovites" are similar to Bavarian creams, except that they are usually made in a hexagonal mould with a hinged lid, as they are embedded in crushed ice and salt. Other preparations such as jellies and "moscovite aux fruits" are often flavoured with liqueurs. The name "moscovite" is often used to describe a selection of "canapés", although strictly a "canapé moscovite" is prepared using a slice of black rye bread, spread with horseradish butter; a border of lobster butter is piped around the edge, the centre is filled with caviar, decorated with shrimps in the form of a rosette. The term also applies to a cold salmon in aspic garnished with Russian salad, artichokes and caviar.

Mousquetaire (à la). This title suggests that a dish is highly flavoured or spicy, an allusion to the lusty behaviour of the musketeers. A "sauce" and a method of preparing lamb cutlets are known by this name.

Moussaka. A dish which originated in Rumania. A charlotte mould is lined with the skins of egg-plants. The pulp of the egg-plants is chopped and mixed with chopped, lean, cooked mutton, finely chopped onion, roughly chopped raw mushrooms, garlic, chopped parsley, tomato purée and seasoning. This mixture is bound with eggs and a little cold demi-glace and placed in the mould in alternate layers with rondels of fried egg-plants. The top is covered with the remaining egg-plant skins and the "moussaka" is cooked in a bain-marie for 1 hour. When cooked it must be allowed to stand for a few minutes before turning it out; it is sprinkled with chopped parsley.

Nage (à la). A method of preparing certain shellfish, particularly freshwater crayfish, small lobsters and spiny lobsters. They are cooked in a "court bouillon", flavoured with herbs. Shellfish prepared in this way may be eaten hot or cold and are served in some of the cooking liquor.

Nantaise. This comes from the French town of Nantes which is renowned for the excellent quality of its ducks. Very often Nantes duckling appears on French menus simply as "nantais". A garnish "nantaise" suitable for large joints of meat is composed of glazed turnips, peas and mashed potatoes.

Nantua (à la). This name is given to various fish dishes, all of which are garnished with crayfish tails, or include a purée of crayfish or a sauce prepared from crayfish, a "sauce nantua". Nantua is a locality in the Department of Ain in France where rivers and streams have an abundance of crayfish.

Napolitaine (à la). Neapolitan style. This title refers mainly to a method of preparing spaghetti which is used as a garnish or served as a farinaceous dish. The spaghetti is bound with a tomato sauce with the addition of cheese and "tomate concassée". The name also applies to a tri-coloured ice-cream made in a brick form or as a gateau.

Niçoise (à la). This derives from Nice, a resort on the French Riviera. The main characteristic of dishes prepared "à la niçoise", is that they include tomatoes in the ingredients. Oil and garlic are also featured in many dishes with this name.

Nivernaise (à la). A garnish of glazed turned carrots and turnips, braised lettuce, glazed button onions and boiled potatoes is served with entrées "à la nivernaise". The ancient province of Nivernais, now the Nièvre Department of France, is well known for the flavour of its vegetables, hence the name of this garnish. A "sauce nivernaise" is a "sauce allemande" garnished with finely shredded carrots.

Normande (à la). Normandy style. This name implies that apples or the flavour of apple has been introduced into the dish. Normandy apples have a great reputation, so also has the cider and calvados (cider spirit) produced there. In many specialities of this region calvados is used in the finishing of sauces. "Sole à la normande" and other fish dishes are exceptions to the usual interpretation of "normande". Another distinctive feature of a large number of Normandy dishes is that they are cooked in cream.

Norvégienne (à la). Norwegian style. This name is applied to a method of presenting cold fish, for example salmon, lobster or spiny lobster. The term also describes certain sweet preparations most of which contain meringue. The best known is "Omelette à la norvégienne" which consists of ice-cream on a bed of genoese sponge, coated with meringue, decorated and quickly coloured in the oven.

Orientale (à l'). This means from the Orient or the East. The term is applied to the preparation of fish, meat, poultry, eggs or vegetables, which are cooked with tomatoes and flavoured with garlic, saffron and, in some cases, curry powder. A pilaff of rice with saffron flavour is often included, i.e. "poularde à l'orientale". The garnish for large joints of meat consists of half tomatoes filled with "riz à la grecque" and croquettes of sweet potatoes.

Orléanaise (à l'). A garnish of braised endive and "pommes maître d'hôtel", made in individual dishes is served with large joints. A "poulet sauté à l'orléanaise" is garnished with turned mushrooms and glazed button onions, red wine is used for the sauce. The region of Orleanais is renowned for the excellent game "pâtés" produced there and for its puff pastries with almonds, notably "Gâteau Pithivier", which takes its name from a town in this district. Orleans is also famous for its wine vinegar, produced there for centuries.

Orly (à l'). A method of preparation applied mainly to fish. The fish is filleted, skinned and marinaded in oil with seasoning, lemon juice and chopped parsley. It is then lightly floured, dipped in a yeast batter and deep fried. Tomato sauce is always served separately. This method of cooking is also used for thin slices of meat or more especially "suprêmes" of chicken. Orly—ancient community of Seine Dep.

Ostendaise (à l'). This derives from the Belgian town of Ostend. This term describes a method of preparing fish, particularly fillets of sole and scallops. Oysters are included in the garnish of both these dishes.

Palermitaine (à la). This comes from Palermo. It describes a method of preparing eggs in a mould, with tongue and truffles, served on a tartlet filled with creamed macaroni. I have seen a garnish with this name served with escalopes of veal. This garnish, which is not mentioned in Saulnier's *Le Répertoire de la Cuisine*, consisted of noodles in butter, with a "julienne" of ham and tongue added.

Parisienne (à la). Parisian style. A surname applied to various dishes, made of meat or poultry in which the garnishes vary considerably but usually include "pommes parisienne". The term also applies to various types of sweets.

Parmesane (à la). A term applied to numerous dishes, which invariably include grated Parmesan cheese. "Parmesane" comes from the Italian town of Parma.

Paysanne (à la). A garnish of carrots, turnips, onions and celery (cut into small neat pieces), lardons and "pommes cocotte" is served with "entrées" with this surname. "Paysanne" is also used to describe a method of cutting vegetables into very neat pieces, either in the shape of sixpences, squares or triangles, which are used in various dishes. This is contradictory to the original interpretation of "à la paysanne" which implied that a dish was prepared peasant's fashion or in a homely manner.

Périgourdine (à la). All dishes with this designation include truffle and sometimes foie-gras in the ingredients. A "sauce périgourdine" is a demi-glace to which is added a purée of goose liver and a dice of truffles. A "sauce périgueux" is a demi-glace flavoured with essence of truffles and garnished with chopped truffles. The truffles of Périgord and Lot are renowned for their excellence. Périgord and Lot are districts in the ancient French province of Guyenne, where excellent "pâtés" of goose and duck livers are also made.

Piémontaise (à la). Associated with Piédmont, an Italian province famous for its white truffles. A "risotto à la piémontaise" is garnished with sliced mushrooms, "tomate concassée" and slices of Piédmont truffles. It is served as a farinaceous dish, or used to garnish meat and poultry.

Pilaff, Pilau, Pilaw. A method of cooking rice, for which Patna rice is the most suitable variety. The rice is cooked in the oven, in double its volume of chicken stock, with finely chopped onion, butter, seasoning and a faggot for approximately 18 minutes. A "riz pilaff" is used in numerous garnishes.

47

Pissaladière. A type of flan, popular in the Nice region. The filling is made with onions, tomatoes, anchovies and black olives.

Pistache (en). This term is used in the south-western part of France to describe a method of preparing a leg of mutton, partridges or pigeons. The outstanding feature of a dish prepared in this manner is that its only garnish consists of cloves of garlic.

Poché. This means poached. Poaching is a very gentle simmering in liquid, the amount and type varies according to the nature of the food being cooked. It is usually considered that the minimum amount necessary to cook the food should be used.

Poêlé. Poêlé is from "Poêlage", often referred to as pot-roasting. "Poêlage" is a method of cooking good-quality meat or poultry in a covered pan on a bed of root vegetables with butter. The butter alone supplies the element for basting during the cooking, liquid should not be added. The lid may be removed at the end of the cooking process to allow the joint to colour.

Polonaise (à la). Polish style. This title usually signifies that beetroot and cream are featured, for example a Polish soup known as "Bortsch à la polonaise". Exceptions to this are asparagus or cauliflower "à la polonaise". In this case, these vegetables, when cooked, are sprinkled with a mixture of breadcrumbs browned in butter, sieved hard-boiled eggs and chopped parsley.

Portugaise (à la). Portuguese style. This name usually indicates that tomatoes, onions or oil are featured. Tomatoes are often predominant, i.e. "sauce portugaise". The garnish for "entrées" consists of stuffed tomatoes and "pommes château".

Primeur. This name implies that items of food are included which are "forced", in order to be enjoyed out of their usual season, i.e. young carrots, turnips, beans, peas, strawberries and tomatoes. The term applies mainly to a vegetable garnish served with "entrées", for example, oxtail—"Queue de bœuf aux primeurs".

Printanier. This term describes a mixture of vegetables, cut in various ways which are used to garnish "entrées", for example, "Navarin d'agneau printanier". Strictly, the term "printanier" from "Printemps"—Spring—implies that the vegetables used are early spring vegetables.

Provençale (à la). A description applied to several preparations which are characterized by the use of tomatoes, garlic, onion or olive oil and in some cases by garlic alone. Provençale comes from Provence, a part of France rich in culinary specialities, most of which include garlic. Olives are also included in some dishes with this designation, i.e. "Sauté de veau provençale".

Romaine (à la). Roman style. This title relates to a method of preparing "gnocchi", for which an explanation was given in Chapter 2. The garnish for large joints of meat comprises tartlets filled with "gnocchi à la romaine" and moulds of spinach bound with a chicken farce.

Rôti(e). This means roasted from the verb "rôtir"—to roast. This is a method of cooking on a spit, by direct heat or in an oven by radiant heat. The distinctive feature of this form of cooking by concentration (which takes place by transmission) is that the internal juices of the food are preserved.

Russe (à la). Russian style. Some dishes with this name are characterized by the use of sour cream, i.e. "Bortsch à la russe". Another example is "Bitok à la russe", in which the "bitok" is coated with a "sauce smitaine". The term may also indicate that caviar is among the ingredients of a dish.

Saint-Germain. The name of a thick soup made with fresh peas, i.e. "Crème St. Germain", which was invented in Paris. St. Germain, a town in the neighbourhood of Paris, is also the name of a garnish which includes peas.

Sarladaise (à la). This derives from Sarlot, a small town in the south of France noted for the truffles found there. The garnish "sarladaise" is prepared from slices of potatoes and slices of truffle cooked in the same manner as "pommes boulangère".

Sauté. "Sauté" is from the culinary term "sauter", which means to cook in fat in a frying pan or a sauté pan over a strong heat. The pan is shaken during the cooking, tossing the food or

49

causing it "to jump", hence the use of the word "sauter", i.e. "pommes sautées". A "sauté" refers to another method of cooking of poultry and cuts of meat which must be of first-class quality. The meat or poultry is cooked in butter or oil in a sauté pan, then removed and kept warm whilst the sauce is prepared. The pan in which the food is cooked is swilled out with wine, stock, etc., this is an important part of the preparation of the sauce. The meat and the sauce should only be combined for serving, i.c. "Poulet sauté Chasseur".

Savoyarde (à la). This is associated with Savoy, a region of France which produces excellent cheeses and where "gratin" dishes are relished. An example is "pommes savoyarde" in which the sliced potatoes are cooked in "consommé" with gruyère cheese in an earthenware dish in the oven. An "omelette savoyarde" is a flat omelette garnished with "pommes sautées" and gruyère cheese.

Soissonnaise. A soup, "purée soissonnaise", and a garnish are characterized by the use of haricot beans as the principal ingredient. Soissons is a small town near Paris which is renowned for the quality of a variety of white beans grown there.

Strasbourgeoise (à la). A garnish which is served with large pieces of meat is known by this name. It comprises sauerkraut, bacon and slices of "foie-gras". The sauerkraut of Strasbourg and the "pâté de foie-gras" with truffles, are well known for their excellence and are rated highly among the many specialities of Alsace.

Sultane (à la). A name applied to various preparations which include pistachio nuts, usually in the form of pistachio butter, i.e. "Velouté de volaille à la sultane". The term also refers to sweet preparations, for example "Abricots à la sultane", in this case pistachio ice is used.

Terrapène. Terrapin. A small American turtle which is not often used in this country.

Tortue. Turtle. This is a general term for reptiles with bodies encased in a bony carapace. There are land turtles, i.e. terrapin, and water turtles, both of which can be eaten, but it is the water turtle which is used for the famous turtle soup. "En tortue" implies that a turtle garnish or flavour is featured, i.e. "Tête de veau en tortue".

Trianon (à la). This term usually refers to a dish containing three colours, i.e. "Consommé trianon", which is garnished with "royale" of three colours and flavours.

Truffé. This means garnished with truffles, i.e. truffled pullet—"poulet truffé rôti".[1]

Turque (à la). Turkish style. Rice is usually a distinctive feature of dishes with this designation.

Tyrolienne. A garnish, consisting of fried onion rings and "tomate concassée" applicable to small cuts of meat which are grilled. A "sauce tyrolienne" is a "sauce choron" with oil used in the preparation.

Vichy (à la). A method of preparing carrots which are served as a vegetable or used as a garnish for "entrées". The carrots are thinly sliced in rings about the size of a shilling. They are cooked in water with salt, sugar and butter until the liquid is reduced, leaving them glazed. Sometimes Vichy water, a mineral water from Vichy, the famous French spa, is used for the cooking of these carrots.

Viennoise (à la). A garnish which is served with large joints of meat or poultry consisting of braised celery, boiled potatoes and "croustades" filled with spinach. The term also applies to a method of preparing veal escalopes. These are egg and bread-crumbed, shallow fried and garnished with a slice of lemon, olive, anchovy fillet, capers, hard-boiled egg and chopped parsley. The escalope may also be dipped in batter and deep-fried. "Pigeon à la viennoise" is cut in four, dipped in egg and breadcrumbs and deep-fried; it is garnished with lemon and fried parsley.

Xeres (vin de). Sherry. A Spanish strong wine with aromatic flavour; so called from Xeres, a place near Cadiz.

[1] Escoffier, Auguste, *A Guide to Modern Cookery*, Heinemann, London.

CHAPTER 4

Designations Relating to Personalities, Historical Events, Clubs, Hotels and Restaurants

A FASCINATING aspect of menu terminology is the study of the many appellations used, relating to royalty, famous statesmen, composers, artists, musicians, personalities of the stage, gastronomes and prominent people from various other spheres. In some instances dishes have been named long after an event or the death of the person commemorated.

In addition to the names of personalities, other factors have influenced the naming of dishes. The names of historical events, battles for example, are often included in a menu. These were originally named either to commemorate a victory or because a particular dish was created at the time of the battle. Marengo is a good example of this sort. Shortage of ingredients at the scene of the battle is thought to have inspired Dunand, Napoleon's chef, to improvise a dish which has become a lasting reminder of the battle and a part of the classical repertoire. The names of famous generals and other distinguished people involved in historical events are another source from which many names of dishes have come.

The custom of dedicating dishes was particularly prevalent from the middle of the eighteenth century until the beginning of the First World War. Auguste Escoffier played a major part in creating dishes, also adapting and naming existing ones. Among the people to whom he dedicated his creations were such famous people of the time as Madame Melba and Sarah Bernhardt.

Although there are some cases where a chef has "named" his creations after himself, the comparative rarity of these dishes in the whole classical repertoire suggests that the creative chef has preferred to dedicate his work to other people, special occasions and places. This is readily illustrated by numerous dishes, named after the establishments where they were originally created and, though now in completely general use, still bear the name of the hotel, club or restaurant with which they were first associated. "Côtelettes d'agneau Réforme" is a good example of this kind.

The development of the classical repertoire has been very gradual. The useful purpose which these many names serve when describing dishes has been mentioned previously. This section of the book is concerned with an examination of examples of the various classes of dish names which I have outlined. Unfortunately there are very few works which deal with this particular subject. In many cases the origin of the name of a dish is very uncertain and it is only possible to give the alternative reasons for them. In some instances I have not been able to suggest why a dish is so called; in these cases I have had to confine the information to that actually concerning the names used. The reader will find further information concerning the composition of most of the garnishes which are mentioned in this chapter by referring to Saulnier's *Répertoire de la Cuisine*.

Agnès Sorel. Also known as "Dame de Beauté", she was the mistress of King Charles VII of France from 1444 to 1450. During this period the King's increased interest in the affairs of his country is thought to have been largely due to Agnès Sorel. Taillevant, chef to Charles VII, created a soup, an omelette, a chicken dish and a method of preparing veal. A feature of all these dishes, which were adapted by Escoffier, is the inclusion of mushrooms.

Aïda. Aïda is a famous opera composed by Guiseppe Verdi (1813–1901) who was a regular patron of the famous Maison-Dorée restaurant in Paris. The creations of the celebrated chef Casimir-Moisson, which he named "Aïda" in Verdi's honour, were "Tubot Aïda", a mixed salad and a "bombe".

Aiglon. This description was based upon a nickname given to the son of Napoleon I and Marie Louise of Austria. Napoleon I was himself likened to an eagle. Laguipière, chef to the Emperor, created a dish of sole, an iced "bombe" and a sweet which are known by this name.

Albert. Francatelli, chef to Queen Victoria, created a sauce and a pudding, which he dedicated to Albert, the Prince Consort.

Albuféra. Dishes with this name are chiefly characterized by the sauce which accompanies them. Marshal Suchet was made "Duc d'Albuféra" in 1812 after the victory in Spain at Valencia near which the lake "Albuféra" is situated.

Alexandra. Many dishes bear this name, all of which were dedicated to Queen Alexandra, wife of King Edward VII. Most of them were created by Escoffier and Ménager, chef to the Royal Household. These include a garnish for "tournedos", a sole dish, chicken dishes and two cold sweets. A feature of most of these is the inclusion of points of asparagus as part of the garnish.

Alice. A method of preparing sole and a sweet were created by Escoffier. He "named" them after Princess Alice, Countess of Athlone, sister of King Edward VII.

Alphonse XIII. King of Spain. Escoffier created a dish using fillets of sole and a method of preparing a "poularde" in his honour.

d'Antin. A renowned restaurant in Paris after which a poached-fish preparation is named.

d'Arenberg. Charles Victor, Prince d'Arenberg of Belgium. His chef, Albert Chevalier, created and dedicated the following dishes to His Royal Highness: a consommé, a garnish for "tournedos" and a pear sweet.

Bagration. The name of a Russian general, Prince Pierre Bagration (1765–1812), who fought against Napoleon. It is applied to various dishes, notably a soup created by Carême.

Baron Brisse. A writer and famous gastronome whose name describes a method of preparing red mullet, fillets of sole and a garnish for small cuts of meat.

Beauharnais. Empress Josephine, first wife of Napoleon Bonaparte. Her name applies to various dishes; among them is a garnish for "tournedos".

Beauvilliers, Antoine. A great "cuisinier", who opened one of the first restaurants in Paris in 1782 called "La Grande Taverne de Londres". He was for a time chef to Louis XVI, and wrote *L'Art du Cuisinier* which was an authoritative standard work of that period. A garnish applicable to large joints of braised meats takes its name from him.

Béchamel. The name of a basic white sauce, the invention of which is often attributed to Louis de Béchameil, Lord Steward of Louis XVI's household. "Béchamel" sauce is believed to have existed for a long time under another name; it is probable that the sauce was perfected by a court chef and dedicated to Béchameil as a compliment.

Belle-Gabrielle. The name given to a chicken "consommé" and a chicken "sauté", created by La Varenne, chef to Henry IV of France, to honour Gabrielle d'Estrées, a mistress of the King.

Belle-Hélène. The name of a famous opera composed by Offenbach. A garnish which is served with large joints of meat, and several other dishes have this designation.

Berchoux, Joseph. A French poet and gourmet who wrote a poem entitled "Gastronomie", which brought him fame. A pheasant dish and a consommé have the name "Berchoux".

Bignon, Louis. One of the greatest restaurateurs of the nineteenth century who became famous owing to his association with the renowned "Café Riche" in Paris. An egg dish is named after him.

Boïeldieu, François Adrien. A French composer who developed comic opera into an early form of romantic opera (*La Dame Blanche*). Between 1804 and 1810 he was Chapel-Master and Director of the Opera in St. Petersburg. Dishes with this name are believed to have been created by Carême and include: a consommé, a sole dish and a method of preparing "Poularde".

Brillat Savarin (1755–1826). A French magistrate, politician and gastronome who is particularly famous for a gastronomical work entitled *Physiologie du Gout*. His name was also given to a rich yeast cake, first made by Jean-Julien; eventually the "Brillat" was dropped and it became known as "Savarin".

Carême created a garnish, an omelette, and a salmon dish in his honour.

Cambacères, Jean-Jacques, Regis de (1753–1824). Cambacères was the Second Consul appointed by Bonaparte. He then became High Chancellor of the Empire and later was made Duke of Parma. He is said to have been a great gourmet, although rather eccentric. He compiled the menus himself for the elaborate dinners which he gave. Of the dishes which have been named after him, a method of preparing salmon trout is probably the best known. A "crème Cambacères" is a rich creamy soup of pigeon and crayfish flavour, garnished with pigeon "quenelles" and dice of crayfish tails.

Carême (Marie Antoine), Antonin (1784–1833). Carême became one of the most illustrious chefs of all time, after a very humble beginning. He was the author of *Le Maître d'hôtel français, Le Pâtissier Royal Parisien, Le Cuisinier, L'Art de la Cuisine au dix-neuvienne siècle* and other books. He is regarded by many as the founder of classic French cookery owing to his practical and theoretical work. There are many dishes which he invented, some of which bear his name, among them are: "Bécasse Carême" and "Perdreau Carême". Carême was chef to: Prince Talleyrand, Emperor Alexander I of Russia, the Prince Regent, later George IV of England, the Bagration Household and Baron de Rothschild.

Châteaubriand. Viscount François Châteaubriand was the French Ambassador to England and a famous gourmet. A method of preparing part of a fillet of beef was invented by his chef, Montmireil, and named in Châteaubriand's honour.

Choron. Alexander Etienne (1772–1834). The name of a French musician who composed several overtures. He was Director of the Paris Opera. His name applies to a sauce, a garnish and a method of preparing "noisettes".

Colbert, Jean Baptiste (1619–83). A statesman during the reign of Louis XIV of France. Various dishes have been named after him of which the best known are "Sole Colbert" and a "consommé". The name often indicates that a poached egg is included in the ingredients of a dish.

Condé, Louis II de Bourbon (Prince of) (1621–86). He was also known as the great Condé. His chef was Vincent La Chapelle who created a number of dishes, some of which were later adapted by Carême. Among the most famous is a "Poire Condé".

Condorçet, Marie Jean, Marquis de Condorçet (1745–84). A celebrated French mathematician after whom a method of preparing salmon is named.

Conti. A famous French noble family, a younger branch of the House of Condé. This name indicates that a purée of lentils is featured either as a garnish for large joints of meat or a soup. The Princess of Conti is credited with the invention of this garnish; it is more likely that the name of the actual person responsible is unknown and that the dish was dedicated to her.

Crécy. Carrots are always predominant in dishes with this name, usually in the form of a purée, notably a soup, "Purée Crécy". There are two theories concerning the origin of the name. The first is that it is due to the excellent quality of the carrots harvested at Crécy, a small town in the Seine-et-Marne department of France. Other authorities insist that it is named after a small town in the Somme, Crécy en Ponthieu, near which the Battle of Crécy took place in 1346 (Black Prince). Monselet wrote a sonnet about this battle entitled "La Purée Crécy".

Cubat, Pièrre. He was chef to Emperor Alexander II of Russia and is believed to have created the method of preparing fish which bears his name.

Cumberland, Duke of (1721–65). An English nobleman to whom was dedicated Cumberland sauce, which is served principally with game.

Cyrano. A consommé, a garnish for cutlets were created by Jules Hépy, chef of the Grand Café de la Paix. He named them after the hero of Edmond Rostand's play *Cyrano de Bergerac*.

Déjazet, Pauline Virginia (1797–1875). A French actress renowned for youthful impressions, after whom a fish dish is named.

Delmonico. The name of a famous New York restaurant which applies to salad and a method of preparing potatoes.

Demi-doff. The name of a princely Russian family. Prince Anatole Demidoff (1813–70) who married Princess Mathilde was a celebrated gastronome. For this reason several dishes were named after him, in particular an elaborate method of preparing poultry.

Diane. A designation which applies mainly to game or suggests a game flavour, an exception being "Entrecôte Diane". The use of the name "Diane" is a reference to the mythological goddess of hunters. It may also refer to Diane de Poitiers (1499–1566) who exerted considerable influence over Henry II of France.

Doria. The name of an ancient Genoese family of nobility. Several dishes have this name, a characteristic feature of them is the inclusion of cucumber in the ingredients. An exception to this is "Noix de veau Doria".

Dubarry. This title signifies that cauliflower is featured either as the main ingredient, i.e. "Crème Dubarry", or as part of a garnish. Comtesse du Barry (1746–93) was mistress to Louis XV. She is said to have worn her hair in elaborate style which could be said to resemble the shape of a cauliflower.

Dugléré. Dugléré, who was chef at the Café Anglais, was responsible for the method of preparing fish (particularly turbot and sole) which is known under his name. He also created "Pommes Anna", a garnish for tournedos and "Germiny en tasse".

Dumas, Alexandre (1802–70). A famous French author after whom several dishes are named. He was also editor of the *Diction-aire de Cuisine*.

Duxelles. Duxelles which is used in many dishes consists mainly of chopped mushrooms. It is believed that "duxelle" was first prepared by La Varenne, chef of the Marquis d'Uxelles. A sauce is also known by this name.

Edward VII (1841–1910), King of Great Britain. A method of preparing "poularde" was created by Escoffier at the Carlton Hotel for his distinguished patron. There is also "Saumon Edward VII", and a sweet (ruche), "Poularde Edward VII", was created on the occasion of the King's Coronation.

Esaü. Lentils are predominart in preparations with this name, notably "Potage Esaü". The use of this name is a reference to Esau, who according to the Book of Genesis sold his birthright to his brother Jacob for some lentil broth.

Escoffier, Auguste (1847–1935). Escoffier had a brilliant career as a chef. He was chef at the Savoy Hotel and the Carlton Hotel for many years. The culinary writings of Escoffier are works of authority; the best known is *A Guide to Modern Cookery*, which was written in collaboration with Philéas Gilbert and Emile Fètu. Escoffier invented numerous dishes, most of which he dedicated to other people. However, a cold sole dish and some sauces bear his name.

Frascati. A garnish for large pieces of meat has the name Frascati, a famous London restaurant.

Garibaldi, Guiseppe (1807–82). A famous Italian patriot after whom a consommé and a type of biscuit are named.

George Sand. The pseudonym of novelist Aurore Dudevant (1804–76) which is applied to a fish "consommé", a sole dish and a chicken sauté, believed to have been created at the Maison Dorée restaurant.

Georgette. A distinctive feature of most preparations with this name is the use of baked potatoes in their jackets.

Godard, Benjamin Louis Paul (1849–95). A French composer of operas, light piano pieces and songs. He was a patron of the Maison-Dorée restaurant, where Cassimir-Moisson is believed to have created a sauce and a garnish which is served principally with sweetbreads or poultry and dedicated to Godard.

Helder. The name of a naval battle between the Anglo-French fleet and the Dutch fleet in 1673. The term applies to a garnish for "tournedos".

Henri IV (1553–1610). Several dishes have been named after King Henry IV of France who married Marie de Médicis, under whose influence French cooking continued to advance, due to the presence of Italian cooks at the Court. A characteristic of most of them is the inclusion of "sauce béarnaise", so named in honour of Henry IV.

Holstein (1837–1909). A German diplomat who was the most important personality after Bismarck in the political history of the German Empire. "Escalope de veau Holstein" is a well-known example of the use of his name.

Jackson, Andrew (1767–1845). A soldier statesman who became seventh President of the United States. A soup bears his name.

Joinville. The name of a French noble family of Champagne. It applies to various dishes, in particular to a sole dish, a garnish and a sauce accompanying other fish dishes. A consommé and an omelette are other well-known dishes with this name.

Joséphine. This designation which applies to a "poulet sauté" is a reference to Empress Josephine (1763–1814) who was married to Viscount Alexandre Beauharnais before she married Napoleon Bonaparte.

Judic, Anna (1850–1911). A celebrated French actress whose name applies to several dishes believed to have been created by Escoffier. Among the best known is a garnish for "entrées", a consommé, a sole dish and a preparation for chicken.

Julienne. The term is used to describe a clear vegetable soup, which was first prepared by Jean Julien, a noted French chef. "Julienne" also describes a method of cutting foodstuffs, particularly vegetables, into very fine strips.

Laguipière. Carême described Laguipière, who was chef to Prince Murat, as "the most remarkable chef of his time" and dedicated most of his culinary works to him. Carême's tutor in all branches of cookery was, in fact, the great Laguipière who died during the retreat from Moscow in 1812. A sauce and two fish dishes are named after him.

Lamballe, Marie Thérèse Louise, Princess of Lamballe (1749–92), was a devoted friend of Marie Antoinette. A cream soup is named after her.

Lavallière, Louise Françoise de la Vallière (1644–1710) was official mistress to Louis XIV. There is a garnish applied to poultry or sweetbreads, an egg dish, a soup and a sole dish with her name.

Longchamps. A racecourse situated near Paris after which a soup is called, "Potage Longchamps".

Louis XIV (1638–1715), King of France, was born at St. Germain-en-Laye, the son of Louis XIII and Anne of Austria. A fish dish and a method of preparing kidneys bears his name. The Court of Louis XIV was brilliant and it was during his reign that the culinary art really began to flourish.

Louis XV (1710–74), King of France. He was the great-grandson of Louis XIV and the third son of Louis, Duke of Burgundy. A method of preparing sole has the designation Louis XV, who took a great interest in gastronomy. He is said to have had a huge appetite, too great for him to be considered a gourmet.

Lucullus, Lucius Licinius (110–56 B.C.). A renowned Roman general who was noted for his wealth and luxurious banquets. Several dishes have this name, most of which require elaborate preparation and include expensive ingredients, particularly truffles.

Maintenon. A mixture known as "Maintenon" is used in some of the many dishes which bear this name, i.e. "Côtelettes d'agneau Maintenon". This dish is believed to have been invented by the Marchioness Françoise d'Augigné Maintenon who took a great interest in cookery. The Marchioness, who was the second wife of Louis XIV (although no written proof of the marriage is extant, that it took place is nevertheless certain), was the founder of a school for young poor girls of good family at St. Cyr.

Manon. A comic opera by Massenet based on the novel *Manon Lescaut*, by the Abbé Prévost. The name applies to a sole dish and a salad.

Marengo. An Italian village, where Napoleon Bonaparte defeated the Austrians in battle on 14th June 1800. According to anecdote, Napoleon's chef Dunand hurriedly improvised a chicken dish on the battlefield, in which, due to shortage of ingredients, he included freshwater crayfish tails and french fried eggs. This rather unusual combination became a classical dish known as "Poulet sauté Marengo". The garnish also applies to a sauté of veal.

Marguéry. A famous Parisian restaurateur who invented a dish known as "Sole Marguéry".

Marie-Louise (1791–1847). Empress of France, the second wife of

Napoleon I. Among the many dishes commemorating her, the best known are: a method of preparing sole, chicken and a "bombe".

Mascotte. An operetta written by Edmund Audran produced in 1880. The designation applies particularly to a garnish served with "entrées".

Masséna, André, Prince d'Essling (1758–1817), was a famous Napoleonic general who was made one of the first Marshals of France of the new régime in 1804. He was also known as "Duc de Rivoli". His name applies to egg dishes, an omelette and a garnish for "tournedos" and "noisettes".

Massenet, Jules (1842–1912). A French composer of comic operas whose name applies to egg dishes and a garnish for small cuts of meat.

Mathilde. Princess Mathilde was the daughter of King Jerome Bonaparte who was married to Prince Demidoff. A "poulet sauté" is dedicated to her.

Matignon (1647–1739). A description of the application of this name was given in Chapter 3. Matignon was a Marshal of France during the reign of Louis XIV.

Maupassant, Guy de (1850–93). A French novelist whose work is distinguished by its universality and purity of style. This designation applies to a cold egg dish.

Maxim. The name of a celebrated Parisian restaurant which refers to an omelette or an egg dish.

Mayonnaise. The origin of the name of this sauce is very uncertain. One theory is that it is a corruption of "moyeunnaise" derived from the old French "moyeu" meaning yolk of egg. Carême suggested in his book *Cuisinier Parisien* that the name of this sauce should be "Magnonaise", a derivative of the verb "manier"—to stir. He considered the name to be appropriate owing to the unremitting stirring necessary during the making of this sauce. Another popular theory is that the sauce was invented by the chef to the Duc de Richelieu after the victory at Mahon (Porte) and that "Mahonnaise" has become mayonnaise.

Médici(s). Two well-known members of the famous Médici family,

Catherine and Marie, both contributed to the development of the culinary art in France. It is not surprising, therefore, to find that their names are included in the repertoire, linked with a number of dishes. It seems probable to me that those which feature "béarnaise" sauce, i.e. "Merlan Médicis" and "Tournedos Médicis", were dedicated to Marie, wife of Henry IV, owing to the connection between this sauce and Henry IV which is mentioned previously.

Melba, Dame Nellie (1861–1931). Helen Porter Mitchell took the stage name of Melba from her connection with Melbourne. "Pêche Melba", perhaps the most famous of Escoffier's creations, certainly one of the most popular, was dedicated by him to honour Madame Melba, an Australian soprano who was a regular patron of the Savoy Hotel.

Metternich, Winneburg, Prince (1773–1859). An Austrian statesman after whom several dishes are named. Prince Metternich claimed that he was instrumental in the arranging of the marriage between Napoleon I and Marie Louise. He was a central figure in European diplomacy of that period, being also known as "The Arbiter of Europe".

Meyerbeer, Giacomo (1791–1864). An egg dish has the name "Meyerbeer" who was a famous German composer.

Mirabeau, Honoré, Gabriel Riqueti (1749–91). A French revolutionist who was a brilliant orator. A rich sauce and several dishes garnished with olives and anchovies bear his name.

Mirepoix, Charles, Duc de (1699–1757). "Mirepoix" is a culinary term said to have been named after the Duke of Mirepoix. It describes a mixture of vegetables, herbs and in some cases bacon, which enhance the flavour of soups, sauces and other dishes. It is usually removed before a dish is served with the exception of "Œuf poché Mirepoix" and "Cailles Mirepoix".

Monselet, Charles (1825–88). A French author and gastronome who is commemorated by numerous dishes. A distinctive feature of them is the inclusion of globe artichokes, truffles with potatoes, fried in butter where appropriate. Monselet's writings include several gastronomic works, the best known being *Almanach des Gourmands*. He also wrote a number of sonnets connected with the culinary art.

Montespan, Françoise Athénais de Pardaillan, Marquise de (1641–1707). The Marquise became a mistress to Louis XIV in 1667, she bore him seven children. A soup and a sole dish are dedicated to her.

Montpensier, Anne Marie Louise d'Orleans (Duchesse of) (1627–93). A garnish and a number of dishes owe their name to the Duchess who was generally known as "La Grande Mademoiselle".

Mornay, Philippe de (1549–1623). A friend and companion in arms of Henry IV, also became known as the "Huguenot Pope". As a protestant he could not accept Henry's conversion to catholicism and was eventually disgraced. This designation applies to a method of preparing fish, poultry, eggs and vegetables which include a "sauce Mornay".

Mozart, Wolfgang (1756–1791). A garnish for "entrées" was created by Vincent La Chapelle to compliment Mozart, the famous Austrian composer.

Murat, Prince of (1767–1815). A Marshal of France who married Bonaparte's sister Caroline, he later became King of Naples. His chef Laguipière is believed to have created the sole dish which commemorates him.

Nelson, Horatio, Viscount (1758–1805). Various dishes are named after Lord Nelson, the most distinguished admiral in English history, who died at the Battle of Trafalgar.

Nemours, Louis Charles Philippe (1814–96). A garnish and several other dishes take their name from the Duke of Nemours, second son of Louis Philippe, King of France.

Nesselrode, Karl Robert, Count (1780–1862). Ambassador to the Tzar. Among the many dishes immortalizing the name of Count Nesselrode, one of the best known is a pudding. This is an iced sweet garnished with "marrons glacés" invented by Mony, the Count's chef. Chestnuts are featured in other dishes with this name.

Orloff (Orlov) (1734–83). A Russian statesman who was a member of a celebrated Russian family. He was Catherine II's lover and the leader of the conspiracy which resulted in the death of Peter III (1762). His name is linked with a number of dishes, some of which are believed to have been created by Laguipière.

Parmentier, Antoine Augustin (1737–1813). An economist and agronomist who popularized the use of potatoes as a food, during the reign of Louis XVI. Parmentier, who wrote many books on food, also invented many ways of cooking potatoes. It is not surprising, therefore, that the appearance of the name Parmentier on a menu indicates the presence of potatoes in various preparations.

Patti, Adelina Juana Maria (1843–1919). A famous soprano to whom Escoffier is believed to have dedicated a chicken dish, an egg dish and an omelette.

Pojarski (1578–1642). A Russian patriot who was head of the anti-Polish movement. A preparation of veal is named after him, i.e. "Côtes de veau Pojarski".

Polignac. The name of an ancient French family dating back to the ninth century. A number of dishes bear this title, a feature of them being a rich creamy sauce garnished with finely cut mushrooms and truffles, i.e. "Filet de sole Polignac" or "Suprême de volaille Polignac".

Pompadour, Jeanne Antoinette, Marquise de (1721–64). A well-known courtesan of the reign of Louis XV. Madame de Pompadour played a considerable part in politics and made herself indispensable to Louis. Various dishes are styled "Pompadour", most of which include truffles in some form.

Rachel, Elisa (1820–58). A great French classical tragedienne who died from tuberculosis at the height of her fame. Her greatest triumph was in Racine's *Phèdre*. Several dishes have been named after her, among the best known is a garnish for "tournedos" and "noisettes".

Réforme. Alexis Soyer, famous chef of the exclusive Reform Club, was a very inventive man. Among his many creations the most famous was the "Soyer" stove which he invented at the time of the Crimean War. This stove became a standard article of service equipment of the British Army. The best known of the dishes created by Soyer is "Côtelettes d'agneau Réforme", which has become a lasting reminder of Soyer's reign at the Reform Club. A feature of this dish is the sauce, which is garnished with a "julienne" of: hard boiled white of egg, gherkins, mushrooms, truffles and tongue. In many establishments a julienne of beetroot is added to this sauce which, in my opinion, is an improvement.

Réjane, Gabrielle Charlotte Réju (1857–1920). A French actress who was regarded by many as the Queen of the comedy stage. Escoffier created a consommé, a sole dish and "œufs à la neige", in her honour.

Riche. It was at the "Café Riche", a Parisian establishment which no longer exists, that a method of preparing fish, particularly sole, was first devised. A feature of this dish is the sauce, i.e. "Sauce Riche". The name "Riche" also describes a method of garnishing small cuts of meat.

Richelieu, Armand Jean de Plessis, Cardinal (1585–1642). He was Chief Minister to Louis XIII and was made a cardinal by Pope Gregory XV in 1622. The name Richelieu applies to several dishes, notably a garnish for large joints.

Robert (Sauce). According to some culinary authors, this sauce which is normally served with pork or fish was invented by Robert Vinot, who is said to have been a celebrated sauce-maker at the beginning of the seventeenth century. Other authorities credit the invention to a restaurateur of the eighteenth century with the name Robert.

Rochambeau, Jean Baptiste, Count (1785–1807). Rochambeau was a Marshal of France to whom his chef Viard is said to have dedicated a garnish for large joints.

Romanoff (Romanov). The name of the dynasty which ruled Russia from 1613 to 1917. The name applies to a garnish for large joints and other dishes. One of the most famous is "Fraises Romanoff".

Roosevelt, Franklin Delano (1882–1945). A salad is named after Roosevelt, 32nd President of the United States.

Rossini, Gioachino Antonio (1792–1868). A famous Italian operatic composer who became musical director of the Théatre

Italien in Paris in 1824. The name "Rossini" is associated with numerous dishes; a distinctive feature of them is the inclusion of "foie-gras" and truffles. Rossini is said to have been very partial to "foie-gras" and is credited with the invention of "Tournedos Rossini".

Rothschild. The name of a great European Jewish banking family. Carême was chef to Baron de Rothschild for seven years and created a "soufflé", an egg dish and a consommé in his honour.

Rubens, Pièrre-Paul (1577–1640). A renowned Flemish painter and diplomat to whom a fish sauce and other dishes are dedicated. Hop shoots are included as a garnish in most dishes styled "Rubens".

Saint-Germain. One explanation of this designation was given in Chapter 3. It may also refer to Comte de Saint-Germain, a celebrated adventurer at the Court of Louis XV.

Saint-Honoré. A "gâteau St. Honoré" is so called in memory of St. Honoré who is considered to be the patron saint of pastry cooks and bakers. The reason for this patronage is not known, as there was no indication of any gastronomical association in his life. (Bishop of Amiens about A.D. 660.)

Saint-Hubert. The application of this name to dishes of game, or those flavoured with game is a reference to St. Hubert, the patron saint of hunters.

Sarah Bernhardt (Henriette Rosine Bernard, 1844–1923). "Fraises Sarah Bernhardt" and other dishes dedicated by Escoffier to her immortal name recall his friendship with this fabulous actress which began when Escoffier was beginning his career at the Restaurant du Petit Moulin Rouge in Paris.

Sevigné, Marquise de (1626–96). A notable French authoress, famous for her letters, the majority of which are addressed to her daughter. The correspondence describes court ceremonies and experiences of that time. Many dishes have been named after her, the best known being a "consommé" and a method of preparing lamb cutlets.

Solférino (1859). A famous battle between the Franco-Sardinians commanded by Napoleon III and the Austrians under Francis Joseph which resulted in very heavy casualties for both sides. Hostilities ceased after a meeting between the two Emperors. The Red Cross idea was born after the battle, inspired by Henri Dunant, a Swiss philanthropist, who persistently campaigned for better care for victims of war. In 1863 a committee was formed which later became the International Committee of the Red Cross, which set out the fundamental principles of the Red Cross. "Potage Solférino", a blend of tomato and potato soup, commemorates the red on white motif of the Red Cross; and the garnish of balls of carrot and potato represents cannon balls. There is also a "sauce Solférino".

Soubise, Charles, Prince of (1715–87). A celebrated epicure who served as a field-marshal during the reign of Louis XV of France. The name applies to dishes which include a "sauce Soubise". This sauce, which may also be used as a garnish, is a smooth onion and rice pulp; it may also consist of a "béchamel" strongly flavoured with onions.

Souvaroff (v), Alexandre (1729–1800). An illustrious Russian general who was noted for his lack of scruples and humanity. A method of preparing pheasant has his name.

Stanley (1841–1904). A Welsh explorer of Africa who is popularly famous for his relief of David Livingstone, but his true importance lies in his discovery and development of the Congo. A feature of dishes with his name is the use of curry powder and cream, i.e. "Poularde Stanley".

Stroganoff (Strogonoff). A name which is popularly associated with a "beef dish", the origin and content of which are often disputed. "Bœuf Stroganoff" is thought to owe its title to a pioneer family of that name (otherwise Stroganov or Stroganow), who were granted land by Ivan IV after the conquest of Kazan, 1552. This family founded iron and salt works and put the conquered people to work in them, under the control of their own private army.

There are many interpretations of how this dish should be prepared and it seems likely that the manner in which it features today is vastly different from the original. However, most would probably agree that the fillet of beef is used, usually the point or foil end of the fillet, either cut in strips or thin round slices. These are seasoned (often with paprika pepper) "sautéed" quickly in butter, removed from the pan and kept warm. The sauce may be prepared as follows: add chopped shallot to the pan, sweat 2–3 minutes, deglaze the pan with vinegar and cream (sour cream is often used) and allow this to reduce, often sliced mushrooms or "tomate concassée" are added. The sauce is corrected and the meat returned to the sauce. There are many variations to the above; in some cases sherry, white wine or lemon juice is used, or the sauce may include a proportion of "demi-glace". This dish has become a popular item for "guéridon" cookery in which case the method may vary from the above, even to the extent of the inclusion of brandy in some establishments.

Suchet, Louis Gabriel (1770–1826, Duc d'Albuféra da Valencia). Suchet was a Marshal of France and one of Napoleon's most brilliant generals. A sauce and a method of preparing sole bears his name.

Sullivan (1842–1900). Sir Arthur Seymour Sullivan was an English composer of comic opera, to which W. S. Gilbert wrote the words. A sole dish was dedicated to him by Escoffier at the Savoy.

Talleyrand-Périgord, Charles Maurice de (1754–1838). A celebrated French statesman and diplomat who was a great gastronome. He had the illustrious Carême as his chef for twelve years, during which time the extravagance of Talleyrand's table was famous. He believed that entertaining was an important element in the success of his diplomacy and intrigue. Several dishes are named in his honour, some of them are believed to have been created by Carême.

Thermidor. The name given during the French Revolution to the eleventh month of the year in the republican calendar. The month fell in the hottest season of the year, beginning on 19th or 20th July and ending on 18th or 19th August according to the year. The most important event that took place in this month was the revolution of 9 Thermidor year II (24th July 1794) the so-called revolution of Thermidor, which resulted in the fall of Robespierre and the collapse of the Terror. The name Thermidor is derived from the two Greek words for heat and gift. It describes a preparation of lobster which is served in the shell, bound in a mustard flavoured "sauce berçy", coated with Mornay sauce and glazed.

Tosca. A successful opera written by Puccini which was first performed in 1900. "Bombe Tosca" is a well-known example of the use of this name.

Valois. The House of Valois had many branches, three of which provided the sovereigns of France. The name applies to several dishes some of which include a sauce Valois (Foyot), i.e. a "béarnaise" sauce finished with meat glaze.

Vatel. A clever and ingenious chef who was employed by Louis XIV of France. He is said to have taken his own life because the fish course for a special banquet was not ready in time. A fish dish is named after him.

Verdi, Guiseppe Fortunino (1813–1910). An Italian composer whose name is commemorated by several dishes; "Tournedos Verdi" is a well-known example. Three of his most popular operas were: *Rigoletto* (1851), *Il Trovatore* (1853) and *La Traviata* (1853).

Victoria (1819–1901). Queen of the United Kingdom of Great Britain, Ireland and from 1876, Empress of India. Several dishes were dedicated to her by her chef, Francatelli.

Villeneuve, Pièrre de (1763–1806). The French admiral who commanded the French fleet at the Battle of Trafalgar. A consommé and a venison dish bear his name.

Villeroi(y), François de Neufville (1644–1730) (Duc de Villeroi). A famous French soldier, a member of a noble family which had risen into prominence in the reign of Charles IX. He became a Marshal of France but was defeated by Marlborough at Ramillies and was relieved of his command. He remained at the Court of Louis XIV with whom his friendship continued. A sauce and other dishes have the name "Villeroy".

Voisin. The name of a celebrated Parisian restaurant, "Pommes Voisin", is a well-known example of the use of this designation.

Waldorf. A famous New York hotel, which has given its name to a salad.

Walewska (i), Marie (1789–1817). A Polish countess who was a mistress of Napoleon Bonaparte, by whom she had a son. A garnish for poached fish is named in her honour.

Wellington, Arthur Wellesley (1769–1852), First Duke of, was a famous English general who defeated Napoleon I at Waterloo (1815). "Filet de bœuf Wellington" was created in his honour.

Xavier, Saint Francis (Francisco de Vasu Y Xavier) (1506–52). A "consommé" and a velouté soup are named after Xavier, who was a Jesuit missionary, styled the "Apostle to the Indies".

CHAPTER 5

Conclusion

THROUGHOUT this book many aspects of menu terminology have been considered and certain points concerning the use of the French language in menu writing have been mentioned. Some reasons for its continued use were given in the Introduction. The value in having a menu with an English translation and description is illustrated in Fig. 1, by the inclusion of an "à la carte" menu from the Dorchester Hotel, London. Specialities of other countries, providing that, in the language of that country, the Latin alphabet is used, should in my view be written as they appear in their country of origin with a translation if necessary.

A debatable issue is whether or not capital letters should be used indiscriminately for names of dishes appearing on menus. One might adopt the view that a name of a dish is a title, as in a book, in which case one could accept the principle that capital letters may be used for all major words. On the other hand, there are those who maintain that to be grammatically correct one should abide by the rule in French that capital letters are used at the beginning of each phrase and for proper nouns. If one takes the view that the latter is preferable then the reader should find Chapter 4 particularly useful, regarding the origins of some of the names which are given to dishes.

Two menus are included (Figs. 2 and 3) which illustrate instances of comparatively recent dedications to personalities. One of these is the menu prepared at the Dorchester Hotel on the occasion of the Coronation of Her Majesty Queen Elizabeth II, in which some of these dishes were specially created and dedicated

POISSONS ET COQUILLAGES

Saumon d'Ecosse Turenne, Poché, Champenoise ou Grillé

Tronçon de Turbot Trouvillaise	21/–	*Turbot on the bone with Seashell food, Mushrooms and Lobster Sauce*
Scampi Mascotte	22/6	*Scampi with Tomatoes, Artichoke and Potatoes*
Filet de Turbot Dugléré	21/–	*Fillet of Turbot with Tomato, Parsley, Shallots and White Wine Sauce*
Vol au Vent de Scampi Newburg	22/6	*Scampi with Lobster sauce in puff pastry*
Tronçon de Turbot Normandy	21/·	*Turbot on the bone fried in Butter with Tomato, Lobster and Egg-Plant*
Truite de Rivière Isabelle	21/–	*River Trout Fried in Butter with Tomato Concassee, Mushrooms, Asparagus Heads*
Timbale de Sole Dorchester	25/–	*Fillet of Sole in creamed Lobster Sauce, Mushrooms, Lobster claw & Pilaff Rice*
Suprême de Sole Louisa	21/–	*Fried Fillet of Sole with Spaghetti, Tomato, Madeira flavoured Cheese Sauce*
Filet de Sole Rochelle	21/–	*Poached fillet of Sole with White Wine Sauce, Grapes & Shrimps*
Aiguillette de Sole Pierrot	21/–	*Poached fillet of Sole with White Wine Sauce, Mushrooms, Asparagus Tips & Breadcrumbs*
Crabe à l'Armoricaine	25/–	*Crab Meat in shell, chopped Mushrooms, Curry-flavoured Tomato Sauce*
Truite Vivante au.Bleu	21/–	*Poached live Blue Trout*
Homard Delmonico	35/–	*Lobster with Sherry & Mornay Sauce*
Crêpe de Homard Dorchester	30/–	*Lobster Pancake with Creamed Mushrooms, Lobster Sauce*
Homard Grillé aux Herbes	35/–	*Grilled Lobster with Herbs & Herbal Butter*
Gratin de Scampi aux Xérès	22/6	*Gratin of Scampi, Cream, Sherry Sauce, Pilaff Rice*

GRILLS

Mixed Grill	27/6	Pork Sausages with Bacon	8/6	Filet de Bœuf	30/–
Loin Chop with Kidneys	22/6	Côtelette de Veau	27/6	Châteaubriand (2 cvts)	65/–
Lamb Chop	22/6	Lamb Cutlets	21/–	Entrecôte	27/6
Porterhouse Steak(4 cvts)	105/–	Côtelette de Porc	21/–	Tournedos	27/6

ROTIS

Poulet de Grain (2 *cvts*)	45/–		
Poularde de Surrey à la Broche (4 *cvts*)	84/–	Poussin	22/6
Caneton d'Aylesbury à l'Anglaise (3 *cvts*)	75/–	Aile de Poulet	21/6
Reine de Surrey (3 *cvts*)	63/–	Cuisse de Poulet (2 *pieces*)	17/6

FIG. 1. Part of an "à la carte" menu illustrating the use of translation and description of dishes.

to members of the Royal family. The second was for a lesser occasion, the annual football match between the Dorchester Hotel and the George V Hotel, Paris, for which a sweet was created to honour François Dupré, who had presented the cup for the competition.

Menu

Les Perles Ambrées d'Astrakan

La Tortue Verte des Iles au Tio Pepe
Le Palmier au Chester

La Truite Saumonée Margaret-Rose

Le Suprème de Poulet Elizabeth II
Les Petits Pois Fin Fleur
La Pomme Noisette

FIG. 2. Creations and dedications to personalities featured on the dinner menu at the Dorchester Hotel, London, on the day of the Coronation of Queen Elizabeth II.

MENU

Le Consommé de Volaille Almina

Les Palmiers au Cheddar

★

Sylvaner
1947

Le Saumon d'Ecosse Margaret Rose

★

La Noisette d'Agneau Lucullus

Louis Roëderer
1943

Les Pommes Olivettes

Les Haricots Verts de Jersey

★

La Surprise François Dupré

Les Mignardises

Croizet ·V.S.O.P.

★

Liqueurs

Le Café

FIG. 3. A dinner menu on the occasion of the annual football match between the George V Hotel, Paris, and the Dorchester Hotel, London.

This vast subject of menu terminology is an ever-increasing one, as new dishes for special occasions are still being created, which do not appear in Saulnier's *Répertoire de la Cuisine*. It may be that a book could be written, featuring recent creations after consultations among experts regarding their originality.

Bibliography

Larousse Gastronomique, by PROSPER MONTAGNÉ.
A Guide to Modern Cookery, by AUGUSTE ESCOFFIER.
Le Répertoire de la Cuisine, by TH. GRINGOIRE and L. SAULNIER.
Dictionary of Foods and Culinary Encyclopaedia, by C. HERMAN SENN, O.B.E.
Chef's Manual of Kitchen Management, by JOHN FULLER.
Dictionary of Gastronomy, by ANDRÉ L. SIMON.
Restaurant French, by STEVE COMBES.
Progressive Catering, Vol. 1, by J. J. MOREL.
Haute Cuisine, by JEAN CONIL.
Encyclopaedia Britannica.

Index

INDEX

INDEX

INDEX

INDEX